A GUIDE
TO
FISHES
OF
THE
TEMPERATE
ATLANTIC
COAST

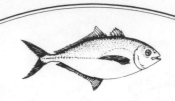

Illustrated with Drawings by the Author

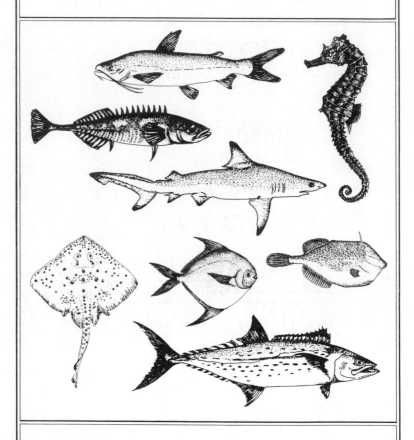

A Sunrise Book
E. P. DUTTON · NEW YORK

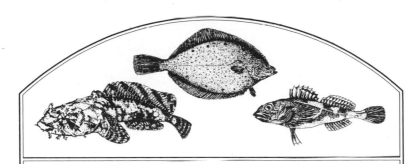

A GUIDE
TO
FISHES
OF
THE
TEMPERATE
ATLANTIC
COAST

Michael J. Ursin

As a guide for certain drawings in this book, when a suitable fish was not available, illustrations by E. N. Fisher and H. L. Todd in *Fishes of the Gulf of Maine,* by Henry B. Bigelow and William C. Schroeder, were consulted.

Library of Congress Cataloging in Publication Data

Ursin, Michael J.
A Guide to fishes of the temperate Atlantic coast.

"A Sunrise book."
Bibliography: p.
Includes indexes.
1. Marine fishes—Atlantic coast (United States)   I. Title.
QL621.U77   1977   597'.092'14   76-30854
ISBN 0–87690–242–5
ISBN 0–87690–243–3 pbk.

Published simultaneously in Canada by Clarke, Irwin & Company Limited, Toronto and Vancouver

10 9 8 7 6 5 4 3 2 1
First Edition

Designed by The Etheredges

To my father,
a sportsman and a gentleman.

THE productions of Nature, as they become less perfect, grow more numerous. When we confider what numberlefs forts have hitherto efcaped human curiofity, what a variety of fifhes are already known, and the amazing fecundity of which they are poffeffed, we are almoft induced to wonder how the ocean finds room for its inhabitants. A fingle fifh is capable of producing eight or ten millions of its kind in a feafon; but Nature has happily obviated this hurtful encreafe, by making the fubfiftance of one fpecies depend on the deftruction of another. The fame enmities that fubfift among land animals prevail with equal fury in the waters, and with this aggravation, that by land the rapacious kinds feldom devour each other, but in the ocean it feems an univerfal warfare of each againft each. The large devour the fmall even of their own fpecies, and thefe, in their turn, become the tyrants of fuch as they are able to deftroy.

Fig. 1. Excerpt from THE NATURAL HISTORY OF FISHES AND SERPENTS, *by R. Brookes, M.D., Vol. III, London, 1763*

CONTENTS

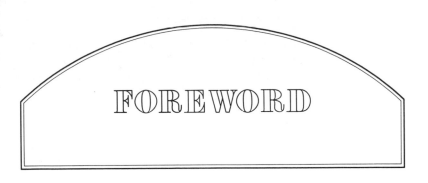

FOREWORD

CHARLES L. WHEELER
Chief of the Aquarium Program
Northeast Fisheries Center
National Oceanic and Atmospheric Administration

In our industrialized society most people live and work far removed from the natural environment of the countryside and the seashore. Less than five percent of Americans are engaged in farming today and relatively few others can be considered as true rural or littoral inhabitants. City dwellers and suburbanites have virtually no contact in their daily experience with the wild creatures of land and sea that basically play an important role in sustaining ecological relationships on our planet.

The ocean, which covers nearly three quarters of the earth, is the home of thousands of different kinds of vertebrates: fishes, whales, dolphins, seals and others, as well as a vast array of invertebrate animals and plants. To know them all is an impossibility, even for a dedicated scientist, but to become familiar with only a few is to appreciate their special way of life and their indispensable contribution to the welfare of mankind. Although the sea may not enter the daily lives of most of us, millions of summer vacationists and recreational fishermen are drawn to the ocean beaches and contiguous waters for a few weeks each year. In responding to the lure of salt water they become acquainted with fishes, often in confusing variety. This immediately introduces problems of identity, edibility and other associated questions: "What is it called?" "Is it good to eat?" "How big does it get?" "Is it common or rare?" and so on.

Familiarity with a few species, unlike each other in many ways, serves to demonstrate the fact that there are many life styles in the sea, as elsewhere, and that each kind of fish is suited to its own particular mode of existence. The points of difference often have adaptive significance which leads to a consideration of, for instance, how and where a flounder gets its food in contrast to the foraging technique of a mackerel, and what characteristics identify the shark as a predator. Although fish vary in their specializations, a closer look reveals that they are essentially similar in general body form and in their manner of breathing, moving about, reproducing and making a success of living under water. Fish and fisheries have a natural and close affinity, a fact that soon demands the attention of the budding ichthyologist.

In this last quarter of the twentieth century the oceans and their living resources are of vital importance in supplying a significant part of the nutritional needs of humanity. As a result of the effort to meet the growing food requirements of a burgeoning population, the commercial fish catch by the maritime nations has more than doubled during the last three decades with a current annual total of sixty million metric tons. To maintain and eventually increase this catch the application of sound management practices is necessary. These involve, among other things, the determination of catch quotas and the extension of the fishery to exploit under-utilized species wherever they may be found. Careful assessment of the year-to-year effects of fishing on the foodfish stocks, and an appraisal of breeding success and environmental conditions at regular intervals, are also among the standard operating procedures.

The trend today is toward unilateral rather than international supervision of fishery resources. The United States entered the field recently when President Ford signed the Fishery Conservation and Management Act of 1976, thereby assuming jurisdiction over thousands of square miles of ocean in which vessels from many countries formerly operated. This fishery conservation zone extends offshore for 200 miles, and foreigners must be licensed and agree to abide by a set of regulations before being allowed to take fish within its boundaries. This is a new venture and several countries with contiguous fishing grounds are now taking similar action. The current rapid expansion of both commercial and recreational fishing is unprecedented and places a serious burden on the existing stocks of fish, both coastal and offshore. The basic management problems are complex but can be appreciated to some extent by those who have had meaningful contact with the marine environment and its inhabitants.

The first step in becoming properly oriented is to get involved with fish and fishing, accompanied by a guidebook such as this which will aid speedy identification and provide details of life history, geographic range, food preferences and other pertinent facts. Michael Ursin has produced a book that will be of great practical value to fishermen, marine biologists, casual seaside visitors and those who have been impressed by the magnitude of the world fishing effort and the need for the perpetuation of the living resource through intelligent management.

C.L.W.

Woods Hole
Massachusetts

PREFACE

A number of years ago while in search of a guide to help me
identify a number of ground fish caught from a small boat, I
was disappointed with the material available. Some books,
though beautifully illustrated and written, contained few more
than the most common species. Others contained an adequate
list of species but were poorly illustrated or contained very limited information about each species. A guide, not too lengthy or
wordy, with accurate illustrations, containing all the fish the
average person would likely encounter, of a convenient size, was
needed.

   A Guide to Fishes of the Temperate Atlantic Coast includes
the common species found from the Gulf of Maine to Florida,
excluding the subtropical seas. Excluded also are the "rare" and
deep-sea varieties that few are likely to encounter except in an
aquarium or museum. The ranges given for the various species
are necessarily approximate, as fishes are known to appear suddenly in places previously strange to them, or to disappear
equally suddenly from their usual range. Weather, ocean currents, and the availability of food are all factors that can significantly alter the usual ranges of fishes. Commercial fishing can
also affect their populations in certain areas.

The sizes given in the text are average adult sizes of the fishes, and the colors given are their usual colors. As with many other animal species, age, diet, and environmental factors can greatly affect the general appearance of most fishes.

The taxonomy, or scientific nomenclature used in this book, is as complete as can be presented without cluttering up the content with an abundance of obsolete terminology. Synonomy (more than one scientific name in current use), when in the author's judgment it is worth mentioning, is given beneath or following the preferred name. The preferred name is generally based on the recommendations of the American Fisheries Society, with only a few exceptions.

The system of classification used is based on the systems developed by Carl von Linné (Latinized as Carolus Linnaeus) in the early 1700s, though today somewhat altered. Latin or Greek words are used to describe particular groupings. The largest group is the kingdom: Monera, Protista, Plantae, or Animalia, the latter of which includes the fishes. In turn these kingdoms are subdivided into phyla, phyla into subphyla, subphyla into classes, and so on, again depending upon external and internal characteristics. Finally the individual animal is given a specific name made up of a genus and species. Because it uses two definitive names this is called the *binomial* system. The specific names are always printed in italics. The following is an example of how the fishes can be classified by such a system, although the system may vary somewhat with different scientists and schools.

The complete classification of the American smelt would be as follows:

Animalia
    Chordata
        Vertebrata
           Pisces
               Neopterygii
                   Salmoniformes
                       Osmeridae
                           Osmerus mordax Mitchill

HOW TO USE THIS BOOK

This book includes a pictorial key starting on page 11 to facilitate the identification of marine fishes. Specimens which are wholly strange to you may be identified by first looking for their general shapes and characteristics, such as the number of fins and their placement or similar characteristics. In each case, certain key characteristics are marked with arrows as an aid to quick identification. When you have found in the key an illustration that most closely resembles the fish you are trying to identify, look in the index of common names to locate the family and specific fish. It should be noted, however, that there are sometimes atypical individuals, such as an occasional accidental cross, and that some species are assigned to families from which they differ somewhat in general appearance.

In the main body of the book, the fishes are presented by order and family in the sequence suggested by the American Fisheries Society.

Preferred common names are given first in boldface type, with vernacular names following them. Though American Fisheries Society has designated the name in bold as the "official common name," a more familiar name is sometimes used in the description. Definitive, scientific names appear in italics below the vernacular names, and are credited to a particular scientist whose name appears in Roman type after the scientific name, *e.g., Osmerus mordax* Mitchill.

Superior numbers after names of fishes or in the text refer to the Notes, which will be found starting on page 239.

Two indexes are provided, one of the common and vernacular names of fishes and the other of the scientific names.

It is hoped that this guide to the Atlantic coastal fishes will be a *vade mecum* for fisherman, student, and layman alike.

M.J.U.

Vineyard Haven
Massachusetts
January 1977

A GUIDE
TO
FISHES
OF
THE
TEMPERATE
ATLANTIC
COAST

Fig. 2. "Snapper"
Juvenile Bluefish

AN INTRODUCTION TO FISHES

Throughout recorded history, fishes have changed little in either structure or behavior. But man's influence has changed their numbers and distribution, and man's knowledge of them has increased a hundredfold.

We have learned of more species, new details of breeding habits and migration, more about the complex food chains that sustain life in the sea. Most important, we have learned that the fishes of the oceans are not an endless resource. On the contrary, species such as cod and haddock, which were once abundant, are now threatened with extinction from overfishing and pollution, as well as from the destruction of the food-producing coastal marshes and the nurseries of fish life on the continental shelf.

The number of different species of fishes is staggering, as is the variety of their size, color, shape, and behavior patterns. Some species are found in nearly every ocean of the world, while others are restricted to highly localized environments. There are fishes that seasonally migrate much like birds, while others remain in the same habitat all year round. A few lead a purely nomadic life.

A fish is generally defined as an aquatic, cold-blooded, gill-breathing chordate with fins instead of limbs. It has a definite brain enclosed in a skull, and well-formed sense organs.

There are two distinct types of fish: jawless fish, consisting of lampreys and hagfish (Class Agnatha), and fish with jaws, consisting of two classes: cartilaginous fishes (Class Selachii), including the sharks, rays, and chimaeras; and bony fish (Class Pisces [Osteichthyes]), which have skeletons made of true bone. Of approximately 30,000 species of fish, about 25,000 are bony and few more than 5000 are cartilaginous.

The anatomical structure of a fish is similar to that of other vertebrates. The vertebral column runs from head to tail enclosing the spinal cord. The muscles are divided into a series of segments, the viscera are contained in an abdominal cavity, and blood circulates throughout the body to supply oxygen and nourishment, and remove waste.

Most fish swim by flexure of their bodies. By successive contractions of the muscle segments, waves of curvature travel along the length of the fish, forcing the water backward, which results in imparting forward thrust to the fish. This motion is obvious in long fish such as the eels. Fish with large, bony plates covering the front portion of the body, such as boxfish, can flex only a small part of their body, the caudal peduncle, and swim by a rapid beating motion of the tail and peduncle. The tail or caudal fin alone is not adequate for efficient swimming, as it is popularly thought to be.

The body of a fish is streamlined so as to allow the water to flow by as smoothly as possible. The slimy secretion on the body is primarily a protective agent and does not serve as a lubricant for ease of swimming.

Skates and rays swim with their "wings," which are actually large, muscular pectoral fins. Some bottom-dwelling fishes may use only their pectoral fins to maneuver about rocks and plants in search of food.

A fish's caudal fin assists in propelling it through the water. The large, fan-shaped caudal fin of salmon or flounder assists in the quick starts necessary to these predatory fish. The deeply forked tails of tuna or bonito offer minimum resistance or drag, a quality important to these fast-swimming species. The heavy, uneven (heterocercal) tail of the shark affords lift to prevent this air-bladderless fish from sinking. Some of the many different shapes and locations of fishes' fins are shown in the accompanying illustration.

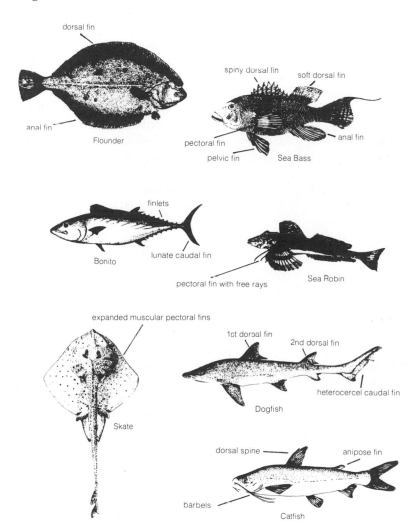

Fig. 3. Shapes and positions of fishes' fins

All fishes in our range are equipped with gills through which blood circulates. The gills absorb life-supporting oxygen from the water, which is combined with the hemaglobin in the fishes' blood. The blood also carries away carbon dioxide waste created by tissue metabolism (cell growth activity). It is circulated by the heart, which is situated in the abdominal cavity behind the gills. A fish takes in water through the mouth, closes the mouth, and forces the water through its gills. Some fishes must swim to accomplish this efficiently. Some will remain stationary when in a strong current to make breathing easier.

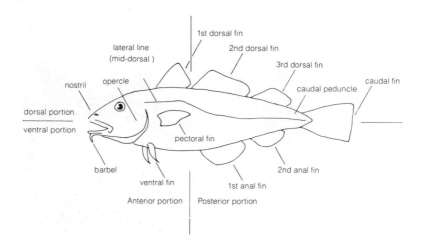

Fig. 4. External anatomy of a fish

A few fishes can absorb oxygen directly from the atmosphere with varying degrees of efficiency. Lung fishes possess a lunglike organ in addition to gills and are the most efficient air breathers. Several freshwater species have other special organs for atmospheric breathing. In our range, the tarpon (*Megalops atlanticus*), though not a lung fish, absorbs atmospheric oxygen with fair success.

The fish's brain, though simpler than that of a mammal, is adequate for all the senses as well as the other physiological functions. All but a very few fishes have a sense of sight through the eyes. Experiments have shown there may be other light receptors on some fish, as, for example, on the tails of lampreys.

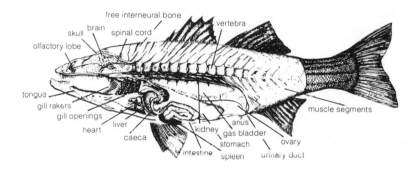

Fig. 5. Internal anatomy of a fish

Fishes have openings at the top or on each side of the snout for scent detection. Sharks and rays, with but one nasal opening, apparently depend on an acute sense of smell to locate prey. Organs associated with the sense of smell are not necessarily localized. As with tasting, this function is performed by the mouth and lips, by the barbels of certain fishes, by the modified ventral fins of sea robins, and even, in catfish, by the skin.

Touch receptors are found over nearly all the skin area. Sharks, for example, have elaborate tactile organs on their fins.

The hearing ability of fishes varies greatly with the species; it is acute and long-ranged in some, very limited in others. Fishes' ears serve to orient them much as our inner ears serve as balance mechanisms. Fish ears also serve as "speedometers," informing the brain how efficiently the fins are being utilized. The air bladders of some fish transmit underwater sounds, acting as sounding boards or "hydrophones."

Unique to the fish is the lateral line. This is visible on many fishes, appearing as a line running from behind the head along the trunk of the fish to the tail. It may be straight, curved, or irregular. A few fishes lack it completely, and in some it is too faint to be discernible. Whatever its shape, the lateral line is made up of sensory cells that detect disturbances such as currents and pressures, and helps orient the fish to its surroundings.

Most fishes have scales. These vary considerably in size and shape. The eel, for example, appears to be scaleless but actually has small, almost microscopic scales. Perch and bass, on the other hand, have clearly visible scales. Scales may also be fused to-

Fig. 6. Placoid scales

gether, forming a shell-like covering, as in the pipefish or sea-horse.

There are four kinds of scales. Sharks and rays have placoid scales.

Fig. 7. Ganoid scales

These are pointed, toothlike scales, giving a sandpaper-like texture to the skin.

Fig. 8. Cycloid scales   *Fig. 9. Ctenoid scales*

Ganoid scales create a hard, shell-like covering, as on some primitive species.

Cycloid and stenoid scales are the most common. Bluefish, scup, bass, and cunner are typical of fish with these kinds of scales.

Hagfishes and some lampreys (jawless fishes) are parasitic. That is, they live off the flesh or fluids of other fish by attaching to them (lampreys) or burrowing into them (hagfishes).

Fishes with jaws have a great variety of tooth forms. Most people are familiar with the long, obtrusive teeth of predatory sharks. Some sharks, however, have teeth that are small and close together, providing only "grinding" surfaces. Some bony fishes have formidable teeth in both the upper and lower jaws, while others have them in the lower jaw only. Still other fishes have teeth that provide abrasive surfaces only, and some are without any teeth. Toothlike structures may also be found on the tongues or throats of some species.

Diet generally dictates the design of the teeth. Predatory fishes have long, sharp teeth to grasp and tear. Shellfish eaters have heavy flattened teeth fused together as plates to crush shells. For feeding on small plankton there are "gill rakers"—long, thin, closely spaced structures set far back in the mouth for siphoning out food.

Fishes have a stomach, liver, spleen, kidneys, ovaries or testes, and intestines. Their digestive process differs little from that of other vertebrates, except that their entire alimentary canal is comparatively short. The biggest difference between the digestive systems of fishes and humans is probably the caecae, or fingerlike extensions emanating from the fish's stomach to aid in digestion. Digestion is accomplished by enzymes secreted in the stomach, caecae, and intestine. Vegetarian fishes tend to have longer intestines than flesh eaters. The kidneys differ in function from those of terrestrial animals by being active primarily in the regulation of the salt content of the body fluids rather than in the elimination of wastes.

In the upper abdominal cavity of bony fishes is the swim bladder. This is a gas-filled sac which can be inflated or deflated at will in order to obtain neutral buoyancy in the water. The fish manufactures gas through an intricate gas-production gland to inflate the bladder. The blood absorbs excess gas to deflate the bladder. Sharks, rays, and skates lack a swim bladder. In order to stay suspended in the water, they must continuously swim.

The body fins of fishes serve to steer and brake their motion, much like the ailerons and rudder of an airplane. To the ichthyologist, fins are an important means of identifying species. Pectoral fins vary most. They may be large and muscular, as in skates and rays, or long and thin, as in flying fish, which actually use them for gliding through the air. Variations in fin movement can be extremely interesting to watch, especially in aquariums, where the fish are close to the viewer.

Almost all fishes are of separate sexes. (There is a perch-like marine fish, not in our range, that is hermaphroditic.) The sex of most bony fish makes little difference in their appearance. (Male and female angler fishes vary greatly, however.) Male sharks, skates, and rays may be identified by external organs (claspers). In bony fish the male has testes (soft roes), while the female has ovaries (hard roes). The female spawns and the male fertilizes the eggs by covering them with milt.

Sharks, rays, and chimaeras copulate, the male introducing sperm into the female by means of the claspers. Either the eggs are deposited in shells (oviparity), develop and hatch in the female but without taking nourishment from her and are live born (ovoviviparity), or they develop within the female with a placental attachment to the mother's uterus, and are also live born (viviparity). Most saltwater bony fish are oviparous.

Nest building is not common with marine fishes. Most find a location well adapted to newly hatched fry. Some lay pelagic eggs that float freely about in marine currents, others lay demersal eggs that are attached to bottom-dwelling plants or to the sea floor by an adhesive secretion. Parental care varies from highly developed (pipefishes and seahorses) to totally lacking.

The largest of all fishes is the whale shark (*Rhincodon typus*), which attains a length of over 50 feet. The smallest is a goby, which measures just over 1 centimeter as an adult. This book deals with neither extreme. It is concerned with fishes as small as whitebait, measuring only a few inches in length, and as large as the basking shark (*Cetorhinus maximus*), which attains a length of 40 feet.

There are two reasons why the size of a fish is an important thing to know in order to identify it properly. First, young fish of some species are given local names which can be misleading to those who are not familiar with the region or species. An example of this is the immature cod, which is popularly known as "scrod." Second, some species have clearly defined differences depending upon age, location, and coloration. An example is the young of the Atlantic salmon, known as "parr" and "grilse."

Because fishes never stop growing from the moment of birth to the time of death, to say that a fish's *average* length and weight are 28 inches and 6 pounds may seem grossly inaccurate to an angler who catches an old specimen that may well be double those measurements.

The natural history of fishes, from man's first encounter with them, has been a fascinating and rewarding study. The greater understanding we gain, the better we can deal with the preservation and conservation of one of the great natural resources of the earth.

*(arrows indicate key characteristics
for ready identification)*

Hagfishes   **Page 30**

Soft mouth; eellike body; one fin on back; barbels on mouth.

Lampreys   **Page 31**

Soft, disk-shaped mouth; eellike body; two separate fins on back; no barbels.

Sharks   **Page 34**

Cylindrical body; gill openings a series of vertical slits; heavy, fleshy fins; sandpaperlike skin.

Skates and Rays   **Page 55**

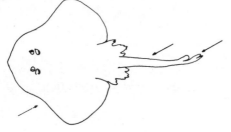

Disk-shaped body, dorsally compressed; long thin tail; dorsal fins on or at end of tail.

Sturgeons   **Page 71**

Series of bony shields on back; long, flat snout; heterocercal caudal fin.

Tarpons and Herrings **Page 74**

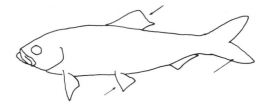

Deep bodies slightly laterally compressed; soft fins; forked tails; large, loose scales; small or no teeth; dorsal fin situated well back; ventral fins placed well back on abdomen.

Eels **Page 77**

Snakelike bodies, slightly laterally compressed; continuous dorsal, caudal, and anal fin; smooth slippery skin.

Anchovies **Page 89**

Small herringlike fishes but with larger eyes and wider mouths; dorsal fin originates behind ventral; rarely exceeds five inches.

Trouts and Salmons   Page 92

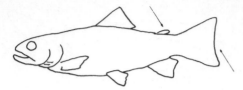

Streamlined bodies, slightly laterally compressed; adipose fin present; soft-rayed fins; almost square tails; smooth or small-scaled skin.

Smelts   Page 98

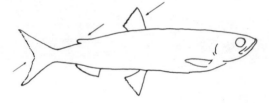

Slim-bodied; deeply forked tail; adipose fin present; silvery sheen or stripe.

Lancetfishes   Page 101

Long slim body with a long, high dorsal fin; deeply forked tail; adipose fin present; large pectoral fin; prominent upper teeth.

Sea Catfishes   Page 102

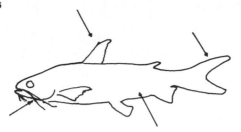

Scaleless, slimy skin; dorsal and ventral spines; barbels about the mouth.

Goosefishes   Page 104

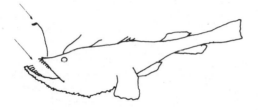

Various shaped fish with gaping mouth; large dorsally flattened head; carries a "fishing rod" on its snout.

Frogfishes   Page 105

Globular body; fleshy fins; laterally depressed; many loose flaps of skin on the body; soft, smooth skin.

Toadfishes   **Page 106**

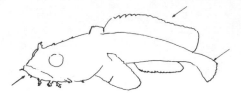

Sculpinlike appearance; soft-ray portion of dorsal fin extends from origin of pectoral fin to base of caudal fin; rounded caudal fin; ventral fins well ahead of pectoral fins; scaleless, slimy skin; gaping mouth.

Codfishes   **Page 107**

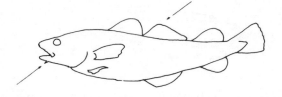

Three separate dorsal fins; smooth, slightly laterally compressed body; barbels on lower jaw.

Hakes   **Page 111**

Two dorsal fins, the second being much longer than the first; long anal fin.

Cusks   Page 116

Long laterally compressed body; long, even dorsal fin; rounded, long anal fin; chin barbel present; smooth skin.

Ocean Pouts and Wolf Eels   Page 118

Eellike body but more laterally flattened; caudal and anal fin continuous; ventral fin very small and ahead of pectoral fins.

Halfbeaks and Needlefishes   Page 120

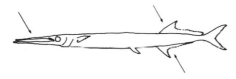

One or both jaws long and needlelike; long slender body; dorsal and ventral fin set well back.

Flyingfishes Page 121

Very large,. winglike pectoral fins; deeply forked caudal fin, lower lobe longer than upper.

Killifishes Page 127

Small, stout body; rounded caudal fin; dorsal fin situated well back; fins soft-rayed.

Silversides Page 130

Small, silvery, large-scaled body; deeply forked tail; first dorsal fin small and placed well back; no adipose fin.

Sticklebacks **Page 134**

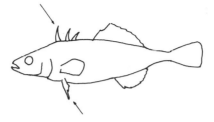

Small fish, rarely exceeding three inches in length; two or more separate spines preceding the dorsal fin; thin, tubular caudal peduncle; rounded caudal fin; spikelike ventral fin.

Seahorses **Page 137**

Horse-shaped head; body covered by bony plates; pipelike mouth.

Pipefishes   **Page 139**

Tubelike snout; long, slim body covered with bony plates; small
rounded caudal fin.

Sea Basses   **Page 140**

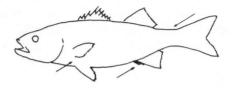

Spiny and soft-rayed dorsal fins, separate or continuous with
deep notch between them; thick caudal peduncle; ventral fin beneath pectoral fin; three spines precede the anal fin; large
mouth; large, distinct scales.

Bluefishes   **Page 148**

Large, blunt head; large mouth with many sharp teeth; spiny
and soft dorsal fin; deeply forked caudal fin; long anal fin.

Remoras   **Page 150**

Large, oval suction organ on top of head; long, slim body; pectoral fin originates at eye level.

Pompanos and Jacks   **Page 159**

Firm-fleshed, laterally compressed body; deeply forked caudal fin; spiny and soft-rayed dorsal fins (first dorsal may be missing or barely visible in older fish) ; one or no finlets present.

Dolphins   **Page 168**

Long, laterally flattened body; high, blunt "forehead"; lower jaw extends beyond upper; one long dorsal fin; deeply forked tail.

Porgies   **Page 169**

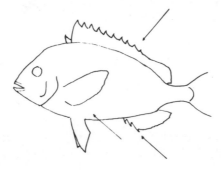

Laterally flattened; large scales; single dorsal fin; long, pointed pectoral fins; anal fin about the same length as the soft portion of the dorsal fin.

Croakers, Drums, and Weakfishes   **Page 171**

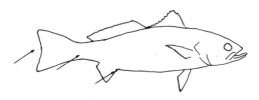

Slightly laterally flattened body; rounded or slightly forked caudal fin; deep caudal peduncle; only one or two small spines preceding the anal fin.

Wrasses **Page 179**

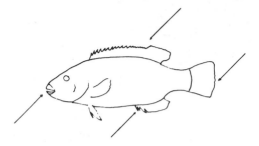

Long, continuous dorsal fin; anal fin with spines; rounded caudal fin; small-mouthed; conspicuous teeth.

Mullets **Page 181**

Heavy-bodied; large scales; dorsal fin about in middle of body; deeply forked tail; broad head; dark belly.

Barracudas **Page 183**

Long, slim body; long head and jaws; lower jaw longer; irregular, fanglike teeth; forked tail.

Wolffishes   **Page 185**

Blunt head; long soft dorsal fin; slightly rounded caudal fin;
ventral fin lacking; large upturned mouth; conspicuous teeth.

Wrymouths   **Page 186**

Slender, eellike body; continuous dorsal, caudal, and anal fins;
lacks ventral fins; mouth opens upward; eyes situated high on
head.

Sand Launces   **Page 188**

Eellike body; long soft-rayed dorsal fin; lower jaw extends well
beyond upper; pectoral fins set low on body; small scales; rarely
exceeds seven inches in length.

Mackerels and Tunas   **Page 189**

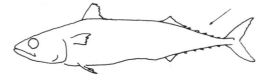

Firm-fleshed, streamlined body; very slim caudal peduncle; separate spiny and soft-rayed dorsal fins; finlets; deeply forked or lunate caudal fin; smooth skin.

Swordfishes   **Page 200**

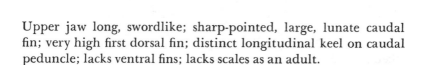

Upper jaw long, swordlike; sharp-pointed, large, lunate caudal fin; very high first dorsal fin; distinct longitudinal keel on caudal peduncle; lacks ventral fins; lacks scales as an adult.

Marlins and Relatives   **Page 201**

Upper jaw swordlike, rounded at the tip; first dorsal high and long; small lanceolate scales.

Butterfishes   **Page 204**

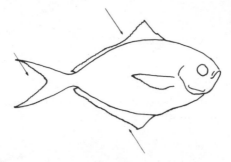

Thin, disk-shaped body; soft-rayed dorsal and anal fin; lunate caudal fin; lacks ventral fins; rarely exceeds one foot in length.

Searobins and Gurnards   **Page 208**

Heavily armored head with spines; large, fanlike pectoral fins; anal fin directly beneath and about the same length as the soft-rayed portion of the dorsal fin; caudal fin straight or slightly forked.

Sculpins   **Page 210**

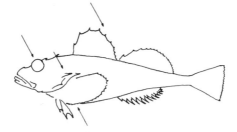

Distinct spines on gill covers and head; large gill openings; large eyes; rounded caudal fin; large, fan-shaped pectoral fins; two large separate dorsal fins; thin caudal peduncle.

Lumpfishes   **Page 216**

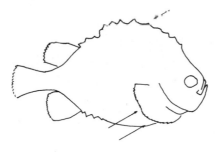

Globular body with lumps; rounded pectoral fin; sucking disk on chest.

Flounders and Soles   **Page 218**

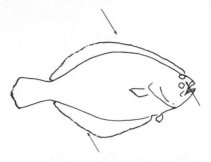

Flat-bodied; lying on one side or the other; both eyes on the upper side; long dorsal fin reaching from caudal to head; long anal fin running two-thirds or more of fish's length.

Filefishes   **Page 229**

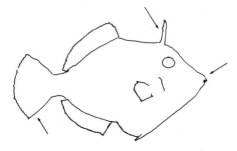

Very laterally compressed body; spikelike first dorsal fin; caudal fin rounded; small, well-toothed mouth.

Triggerfishes   **Page 229**

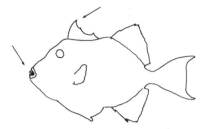

Very laterally compressed body; small eyes; first dorsal fin with
3 erectable spines placed directly over the pectoral fin; second,
soft-rayed dorsal fin placed well back; small, well-toothed mouth;
hard bony scales forming a flexible armor cover.

Puffers   **Page 232**

Head covered with a hard, bony plate; small dorsal fin set well
back; rounded caudal fin; can inflate abdomen when disturbed.

THE FISHES

CLASS *Agnatha (Marsipobranchii)*

ORDER *Myxiniformes* (Hyperotreti, Myxinoidea)
HAGFISHES — FAMILY *Myxinidae*

Hagfish
Atlantic hagfish, slime eel
Myxine glutinosa Linnaeus

SIZE: Eighteen to 24 inches, rarely exceeds 30 inches.

COLOR: Gray to brown, sometimes mottled with darker markings; abdomen lighter.

RANGE: Inhabits large areas of the colder waters of the Atlantic; rarely encountered in depths of less than 10 fathoms.

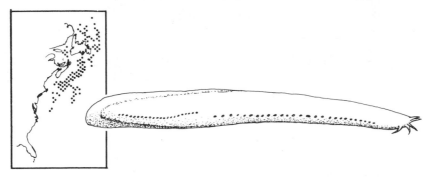

The hagfish or "hag" lacks bones, has a cartilaginous skeleton, is jawless, scaleless, and has an eellike form. It possesses a finlike fold of skin along half its length dorsally and approximately one-quarter of its ventral length. There are several barbels about its mouth and it has several rows of sharp teeth.

Hagfish are known by commercial fishermen for their habit of attacking hooked fish (long-lined) or fish in gill nets, and eating all but the skin and bones. They are not truly parasitic as they do not attack free, healthy fish. They are known also for their distasteful habit of ejecting several quarts of mucouslike material when handled, apparently as a defensive mechanism.

Their commercial importance lies only in their being a nuisance to fishermen.

ORDER *Petromyzontiformes* (Petromyzontia, Hyperoartii)

LAMPREYS — FAMILY *Petromyzontidae*

Sea lamprey
Lamprey, spotted lamprey, lamper, eelsucker
Petromyzon marinus Linnaeus

SIZE: Two to 3 feet long and up to 2½ lbs. Larvae up to 8 inches.

COLOR: Yellow-brown, green-brown, mottled, sometimes so dark as to appear black; abdomen lighter. Young appear a uniform dark gray-blue. Landlocked lampreys may be somewhat differently colored.

RANGE: Known throughout our range.

Sea lampreys are anadromous fish, that is, they ascend rivers from the sea to breed. Eellike in appearance, they have two dorsal fins and a caudal fin, which are actually folds of skin. Their jaws are so poorly developed that they are barely evident. Lampreys use their several rows of sharply hooked teeth to attach themselves to other fish, tearing through the skin and scales to feed parasitically on the blood of the victim. They prey upon a variety of anadromous as well as purely marine species and are strong swimmers.

CARTILAGINOUS FISHES
CLASS *Chondrichthyes (Selachii)*
SHARKS, SKATES, AND RAYS

Only recently has it become evident that many fishes in this class possess sports fishing value and are excellent for eating as well. Many varieties are hated by both anglers and commercial fishermen, as they can and do damage fishing gear. There are too many instances of sharks, when accidentally caught, being viciously beaten and thrown back, particularly considering that many species are harmless and are good to eat. Skates and rays, some of which are excellent food fish, also all too frequently suffer this same wasteful end.

Sharks, skates, and rays are characterized by a cartilaginous skeleton, totally lacking true bone. The gill openings are slits rather than the typical opercula of most other fishes. Fertilization occurs internally. Some of these fishes are egg bearing and others produce live young.

SHARKS — ORDER *Squaliformes* (Pleurotremata)

THE CARPET SHARKS — FAMILY *Orectolobidae*

The carpet sharks are widely ranging, colorful sharks and are harmless unless provoked. The nurse shark represents the family in our area.

Nurse shark
Ginglymostoma cirratum Bonnaterre

SIZE: Normally an 8- to 10-foot fish, but occasionally reaches 14 feet.

COLOR: Brown to yellow-brown above, white abdomen.

RANGE: Florida to North Carolina, occasionally to Cape Cod.

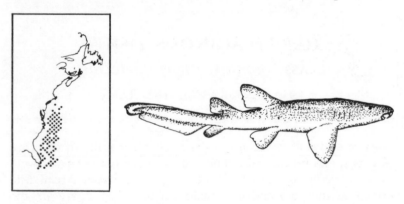

Two large dorsal fins situated well to the back, a barbel at each nostril, and a long caudal fin with no apparent lower lobe distinguish the nurse shark from other sharks in our area.

During the breeding season females have been observed with fins torn and scarred by the male's better-developed teeth.

The nurse shark feeds primarily on bottom life such as crabs and lobsters. It is not sought by commercial fishermen although its flesh is tender and tasty.

SAND SHARKS — FAMILY *Carchariidae* (Odontaspididae)

Sand shark
Dogfish shark, ground shark, sand tiger
Odontaspis taurus Rafinesque
Carcharias taurus Rafinesque
Carcharias littoralis Mitchill

SIZE: Rarely exceeds 8 feet and 200 pounds, individuals 4 to 6 feet in length are common.

COLOR: Many yellow-brown, roundish spots on a gray-brown skin, white or gray-white underneath.

RANGE: Common throughout our range, traveling rather far north in the summer months.

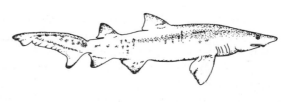

Two spineless dorsal fins of about equal size, a large anal fin and the lack of lateral keels on the caudal peduncle easily distinguish the sand shark from other sharks in our area. They possess sharp, slender teeth. The caudal fin is heterocercal. These sharks prefer warmer climates but will follow populations of fish north to Cape Cod. They feed in the shallows and may even follow food into the mouths of rivers. Their diet is made up of a large variety of small fishes.

They do not show interest in nonmarine species and have never been known to launch an unprovoked attack on a human being. It would, however, be less than advisable to annoy a sand shark, as their teeth are capable of inflicting a sizable wound.

Sand sharks are edible and easily caught with live bait. They are not commercially sought after as there are too few of them to make such a fishery profitable.

MACKEREL SHARKS — FAMILY *Lamnidae* *(Isuridae)*

Mackerel sharks have recently been shown in fiction and on the screen in a sinister role as man-eaters. As such, they occupy in the minds of laymen an unenviable category all their own. In all fairness, however, not all unprovoked attacks on human beings have been by mackerel sharks, nor are shark attacks on humans nearly as frequent as public opinion would have it. The danger of shark attack is reduced in the northern part of our range, as the marine food supply is abundant there and the colder temperatures slow the sharks' metabolism; this in turn reduces their appetite.

There is little doubt, however, that these sharks are potentially dangerous to man not only in the water but in a boat or on land as well, as long as there is enough life remaining in them to lash forth. The great white shark in particular has unquestionably earned its reputation as a man-eater. There is also much evidence that makos have attacked people and small boats. It is known, too, that many other types of sharks are capable of inflicting wounds on people. Nevertheless, if common sense, care, and a little knowledge are used in dealing with sharks, the threat they present to human life under normal conditions is small indeed.

Sharks of this family possess sharp, conspicuous teeth. Their tails are nearly lunate; that is, they have the lower lobe nearly as long as the upper. Gill openings are larger than in other sharks (except the basking shark), and mackerel sharks have an anal fin.

Mackerel sharks are fast swimmers and are able to obtain their food by speed alone. These sharks spend a great deal of time near the surface, displaying the classic dorsal fin. They also dive to great depths in search of many kinds of fish and occasionally marine mammals.

Porbeagle
Mackerel shark, blue dog shark, blue mako
Lamna nasus Bonnaterre
Isurus nasus Bonnaterre

SIZE: An adult fish may be expected to be 5 to 7 feet long and to weigh under two hundred pounds, although larger individuals are sometimes seen.

COLOR: Dark gray-blue on the back and upper side of the fins, white beneath, the pectoral fin usually bordered with a thin black margin.

RANGE: Widely ranging in our area, and preferring deeper waters.

The mackerel shark* is a heavy-bodied shark with a narrow nose and slim caudal peduncle. The pectoral fins are about twice as long as wide; the dorsal fin is nearly as wide as high. The second dorsal and anal fins directly oppose one another. The mackerel shark has smooth-edged teeth. It can be distinguished from the mako by the distinct denticle at the base of each tooth, which the mako lacks, and by a keel on the caudal peduncle which continues well into the caudal fin.

* Though the American Fisheries Society has designated the name in boldface type as the "official common name," this name is, in the author's opinion, still more widely used.

In the open ocean the mackerel shark is frequently seen basking near the surface. Though they are strong swimmers they are easily brought in when hooked.

They primarily eat cod, mackerel, and herrings, though they do not disdain other fish, as well as other sharks.

There is not a great commercial demand for this fish, though its flesh is excellent for eating, having a taste and texture resembling swordfish. It would not be surprising to see these sharks become the object of a commercial fishery in the near future.

Shortfin mako
Sharp-nosed mackerel shark, mako
Isurus oxyrinchus Rafinesque
Isurus tigris Atwood

SIZE: A 12-foot specimen is large, the average being closer to 8 feet.

COLOR: Viewed in the water, the mako appears a deep blue above, white below. The dead fish appears gray-blue to gray above, light gray below.

RANGE: Mostly an open ocean shark, it ranges widely in the Atlantic, preferring the warmer climates, but ranging northward in the summer. It is rarely found inshore.

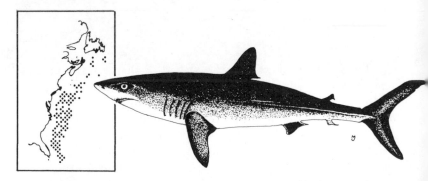

The average vacationer is not likely to encounter a mako. This shark is, however, of interest to deep-sea sports fishermen, as it is indeed a sports fish and fine for eating as well. Its speed places it among the fastest fishes. While feeding or at play, mako sharks may be seen leaping several feet out of the water. They are fearless feeders, reported to attack other sharks much larger than themselves.

White shark
Man-eater, great white shark
Carcharodon carcharias Linnaeus

SIZE: These sharks vary greatly in size depending upon habitat and available food. The largest on record was 36½ feet; 12 to 18 feet would be common. An 18-footer weighs well over a ton.

COLOR: Smaller ones have varying shades of gray-brown above to an off-white below. Larger ones appear lighter in color, frequently a light lead gray. There often is a dark spot immediately behind the pectoral fin.

RANGE: Nearly worldwide in range, preferring the warmer regions; less common in the extreme cold and the tropics.

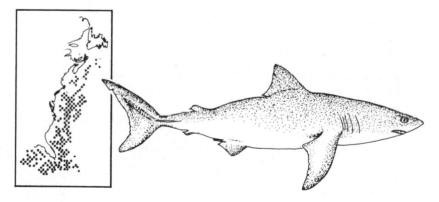

As its name implies, this shark is responsible for the majority of attacks on man and even boats. Attacks are, however, far less common than most people imagine. The white shark's preference for the deeper waters keeps it well offshore, only occa sionally entering shallow waters in well-populated areas, as it is attracted to noises and disturbances in the water.

In the water the man-eater looks very much like a mackerel shark but is somewhat more robust. Any large, actively swimming shark of this general shape should be treated with extreme care. The white shark's teeth are its best identifying mark. They are triangular, razor sharp, and have serrated edges.

Man-eaters are sought for sport, though reportedly they are not as spectacular a sportfish as the mako; rather they are sluggish fighters when hooked.

BASKING SHARKS* — FAMILY *Cetorhinidae*[1]

This family consists of a single species, the basking or bone shark.

Basking shark
Bone shark
Cetorhinus maximus Gunnerus

SIZE: Forty feet long is very large for this fish, although a 50-footer is on record and 30-footers are common.

COLOR: Gray-brown to nearly black above, white below.

RANGE: Cape Cod north to the Maritime Provinces, rarely south of Cape Cod.

* Included in FAMILY *Lamnidae* in some texts.

Second in size only to the whale shark, the basking shark may be identified by its large gill openings, which continue nearly all the way around the neck. These sharks have very small teeth and long, comblike filaments in their throats with which they filter out plankton and small crustaceans for food.

They have been hunted in the past for their oil. Today few commercial fishermen exploit them.

THRESHER SHARKS — FAMILY *Alopiidae*

Thresher sharks are unique among sharks for the unusually long upper lobe of their caudal fin.

The threshers are represented by only one species in our area: *A. vulpinus*. Another closely related species inhabits the Indian Ocean.

Thresher shark
Long-tailed shark
Alopias vulpinus Bonnaterre
Alopias vulpes Gmelin

SIZE: Commonly from 12 to 20 feet long (tail included). Does not often exceed 20 feet in length.

COLOR: Dark brown, blue-gray-brown, gray-blue, sometimes very dark or nearly black above, white below.

RANGE: Occurs throughout our area, but prefers the warmer climates.

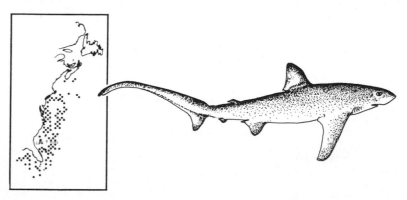

The thresher is not likely to be confused with any other shark. The upper lobe of its caudal fin is nearly as long or longer than one-half of the length of the body and head combined.

The thresher frequently feeds in shoal waters, herding and slashing schools of small fish with its tail, often teaming with another thresher.

These sharks do not under normal conditions pose any threat to people. There are reports, however, of wounded threshers becoming unusually aggressive.

REQUIEM SHARKS — FAMILY *Carcharhinidae*

This family is tropical for the most part but is represented in our area by a few well-toothed, streamlined sharks. They all bear live young.

Atlantic sharpnose shark
Sharpnose shark
Rhizoprionodon terraenovae **Richardson**
Scoliodon terraenovae Richardson

SIZE: Commonly 2 to 2½ feet, occasionally to 3 feet long.

COLOR: Gray-brown or olive-brown above with dark-edged dorsal and caudal fins, white below.

RANGE: Florida to North Carolina, strays to Cape Cod.

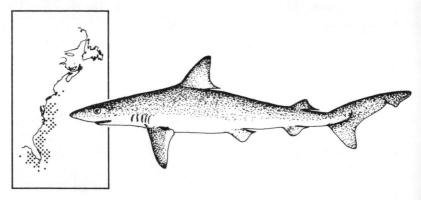

This is a small shark that is easily confused with a young mako, but has a proportionately larger second dorsal and anal fin, and a shallow but distinct furrow or groove from the corner of the mouth to the nostril. The pectoral fin is smaller than it is in most sharks in our area. Its teeth are smooth edged.

Dusky shark
Dusky ground shark
Carcharhinus obscurus Lesueur (*Eulamia obscura*)
Charcharinus laniella

SIZE: Commonly 10 to 11 feet, rarely to 14 feet.

COLOR: Blue-gray to gray above, pelvic and anal fins tipped in white, undersides white.

RANGE: Florida to Cape Cod, occasionally strays as far as Nova Scotia in late summer.

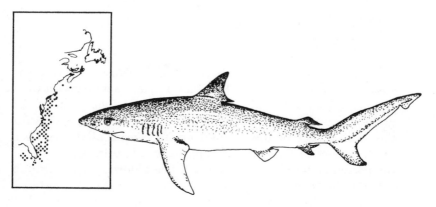

The dusky shark is identified by a small but definite ridge along the back between the dorsal fins. Its first dorsal fin is relatively small, and its teeth are conspicuous and smooth.

This shark prefers the warmer waters and only rarely ventures as far north as the Gulf of Maine. It feeds on fish and squid. The dusky shark is a deep-water fish.

Sandbar shark
Brown shark, New York ground shark
Carcharhinus milberti Müller and Henle[2] (*Eulamia milberti*)

SIZE: Five to 6 feet long, occasionally to 8 feet.

COLOR: Gray to gray-brown, light gray or gray-brown beneath.

RANGE: Cape Cod south.

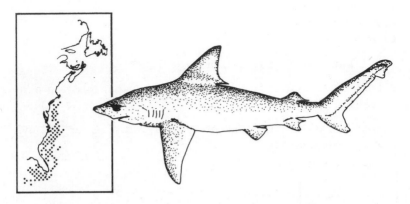

The sandbar shark closely resembles the dusky but is differentiated from it by a larger dorsal fin situated more forward than the dusky shark's in relation to the pectoral fin. The dorsal of the dusky shark originates nearly midway along the body, even with the trailing edge of the pectoral fin; the dorsal of the sandbar shark is more forward, located approximately over the center of the pectoral fin. The sandbar shark has a dorsal ridge running between the dorsal fins.

The sandbar shark is one of the few species of sharks that enter estuaries and rivers.

Spotfin ground shark
Small blacktip shark, blacktip shark, bull shark
Carcharhinus limbatus Valenciennes

SIZE: Normally up to 7 feet in length, though specimens 9 feet long have been recorded.

COLOR: Gray to gray-brown above, light gray to white beneath, dark tips on the fins.

RANGE: A southern shark not often found north of Cape Hatteras, but sometimes straying as far north as Cape Cod in the warmer months.

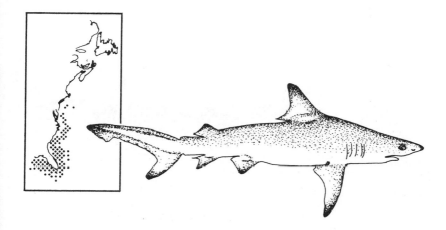

C. *limbatus*'s diet is very varied, including sharks, rays, small fish, and crabs.

The spotfin is a tropical shark that often ranges into temperate waters. It has a streamlined form, with large dorsal and pectoral fins and a fleshy caudal fin.

From 3 to 6 young, less than 2 feet long, are born in Florida waters in the spring.

Tiger shark
Leopard shark
Galeocerdo cuvieri Peron and Lesueur
Galeocerdo arcticus Faber

SIZE: Though there are claims of 30-foot specimens, a 14-footer is a large individual; specimens 10 feet long are more common.

COLOR: Young tiger sharks up to about 7 feet long show dark

brown spots and vertical bars on the top and sides. Older fish are more uniform in coloring.

RANGE: Cape Cod and south.

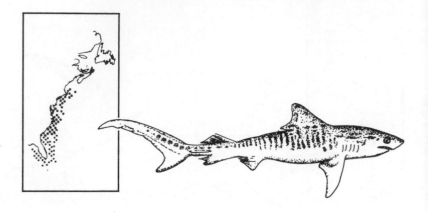

Look for a ridge on the caudal peduncle, a small second dorsal fin, pointed lobes on the caudal fin, and a distinct furrow on either side of the snout as sure identification of the tiger shark.

The tiger shark is a voracious feeder, preying on fishes, turtles, crabs, and, if hungry enough, almost anything. The tiger shark is reported to attack boats, for reasons not currently known. When caught on hook and line, tiger sharks are reported to put up long, vigorous fights. They are feared by man in most areas, though in most cases without good cause.

Blue shark
Blue dogfish, blue dog shark
Prionace glauca Linnaeus

SIZE: Averages less than 10 feet long, a 15-foot specimen is rare.

COLOR: The adult fish is a deep cobalt blue above and white beneath. Upon death it rapidly loses its color, becoming a dull gray.

RANGE: The blue shark is found throughout our range, but prefers the warmer waters.

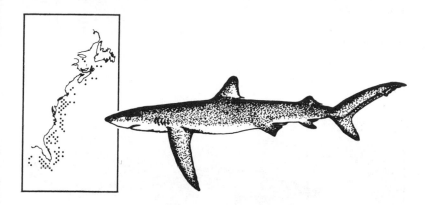

The blue shark has its first dorsal fin placed well behind an unusually large pectoral fin. Its teeth are large and serrated. It is a streamlined fish, and its speed has been recorded at faster than 20 miles an hour.

There are reports of this shark attacking humans, although few, if any, of these alleged attacks have been authenticated. The blue shark has no commercial value, as its flesh is not particularly palatable. The liver, however, is reportedly prized as a delicacy by European epicures.

SMOOTH DOGFISHES* — FAMILY *Triakidae*[3]

These small sharks have only small grinding teeth. They are represented by *M. canis* in our area.

Smooth dogfish
Common dogfish, gray dogfish, grayfish, smooth hound
Mustelus canis Mitchill

* Included in FAMILY *Carcharhinidae* in some texts.

SIZE: Rarely exceeds 5 feet, 3½ to 4 feet long is common.

COLOR: Silver-gray, gray-olive, or slate above, white or cream below.

RANGE: Throughout our range.

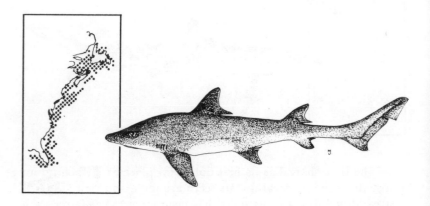

The smooth dogfish is identified by its two dorsal fins of nearly equal size, its soft heterocercal caudal fin and its small grinding teeth.

Although disdained by many fishermen, the flesh of the smooth dogfish is excellent food. Hopefully, someday this harmless fish will, when caught, meet a better fate than to be mercilessly beaten on the head and returned to the water unconscious or dead.

The smooth dogfish is live born. The young immediately begin searching for food.

HAMMERHEAD SHARKS — FAMILY *Sphyrnidae*

These sharks, which are characterized by oddly shaped heads, are represented in our area by two species. Three other species roam the tropical seas.

Bonnethead
Shovel head
Sphyrna tiburo Linnaeus

SIZE: Average 4 to 5 feet long, rarely exceeds 6 feet.

COLOR: Gray to gray-brown above, light brown below; occasionally a few dark spots on the sides.

RANGE: Florida to North Carolina, strays to Cape Cod.

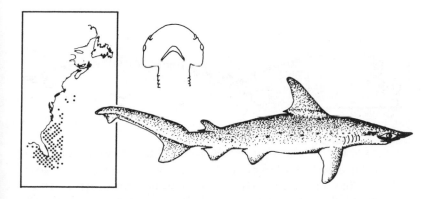

This is primarily a tropical shark that may stray as far north as Cape Cod in exceptionally warm summers.

It is easily identified by a wide head with eyes at the end of large protuberances. Its head is noticeably smaller than that of the hammerhead shark, below.

It is a far more sluggish fish than the hammerhead and has not been reported to be dangerous to humans.

On occasion the bonnethead is sought after by rod-and-reel fishermen, as it is considered to be an excellent fighter. It subsists on crabs, shrimps, and small fishes.

Smooth hammerhead
Hammerhead shark
Sphyrna zygaena Linnaeus

SIZE: Six to 12 feet long.

COLOR: Gray to gray-brown above, gray below.

RANGE: Normally Florida to Cape Cod; encountered on rare occasions as far north as the Gulf of Maine.

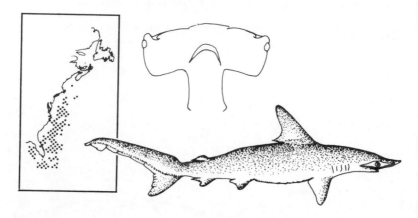

It is unlikely anyone would confuse the hammerhead with any other shark. Its large, laterally flattened head and a noticeably forked anal fin clearly differentiate it from other sharks.

Its diet consists of fishes, including other sharks. The hammerhead is a threat to humans only when provoked.

Hammerheads have been reported to be cannibalistic. In areas where sharks are commercially fished, they are known to attack hooked or entrapped sharks.

Two other hammerheads are found along the Atlantic coast: the great hammerhead, *S. mokarran,* and the tropical hammerhead, *S. lewini. S. zygaena* is distinguished from them by a scalloped outline on the forehead. *S. mokarran* and *S. lewini* have smoothly rounded foreheads.

SPINY DOGFISHES (DOGFISH SHARKS) —
FAMILY *Squalidae*

The chief anatomical characteristic that distinguishes the spiny dogfishes from other dogfishes and sharks is their lack of an anal fin. The most abundant representative of this family in our area is *S. acanthias,* which is found in limited numbers from the coast of Florida north to Cape Cod, and is abundant from Cape Cod to the Maritime Provinces.

Black dogfish
Centroscyllium fabricii Reinhardt

SIZE: Two to 3½ feet.

COLOR: Dark brown to black above and below.

RANGE: Florida to North Carolina, strays to Cape Cod.

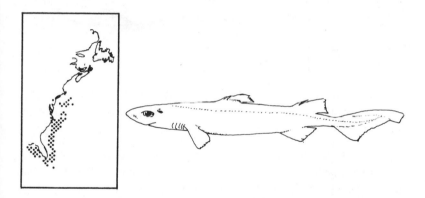

The black dogfish is a deep-water species commonly found in water of 500 fathoms or more—over half a mile deep. Rarely does the black dogfish venture into shoal water. This small shark can be readily identified by its combination of dark color and lack of a first anal fin. Its diet includes a variety of small marine organisms such as cephalopods and crustaceans.

Spiny dogfish
Spined dogfish, piked dogfish, grayfish
Squalus acanthias Linnaeus

SIZE: Two to 3 feet; occasionally reaches 4 feet in length.

COLOR: Gray to brown-gray above, white spots on the sides, gray to white beneath.

RANGE: Southern Labrador to North Carolina, strays to Florida.

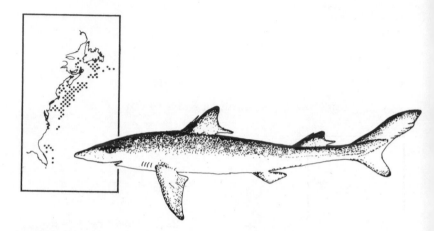

The spiny dog is an unusual shark because of its ability to control its own digestive process, a phenomenon still to be fully understood by the biomedical community.

S. acanthias is armed with a row of small, sharp teeth with but a single point and knifelike cutting edges.

This is a very common shark, and it is often a nuisance to commercial fishermen. Though their flesh is of good food value, like that of many other sharks, it is not often eaten.

GURRY SHARKS — FAMILY *Dalatiidae**

The upper teeth are conspicuously different from the lower in this family. We have in our area the Greenland shark from this group.

* Included in FAMILY *Squalidae* in some texts.

Greenland shark
Ground shark, sleeper shark
Somniosus microcephalus Bloch and Schneider

SIZE: Average 10 to 14 feet long, individuals in excess of 20 feet have been recorded.

COLOR: Deep brown to black or dark gray above, lighter beneath. Dark crossbars may be present on the sides.

RANGE: Canadian waters; occasionally ventures as far south as Cape Cod.

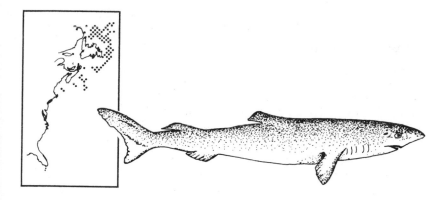

The Greenland shark has conspicuously small dorsal fins and small pectoral fins, and the lower lobe of its caudal fin is about half as long as the upper. This shark most closely resembles the Portuguese shark, which differs from the Greenland shark, however, by having free spines ahead of the dorsal fins.

This is a sluggish shark preferring deeper waters. Its diet is varied, and it disdains little in the way of a meal. It eats carrion and scraps from fishing boats as well as live fish and occasionally seals.

The Greenland shark presents no threat to man. In European waters it is caught commercially for its oil. Sports fishermen avoid it, as it allows itself to be hauled up like a lifeless carcass when hooked.

MONKFISHES (ANGEL SHARKS) — FAMILY *Squatinidae*

Monkfishes are a bottom-dwelling family of flattened fishes with gill slits rather than opercula. There are about 10 species of monkfishes; the only one of these normally found in our range is the *S. squatina*.

Atlantic angel shark
Monkfish, angel shark
Squatina dumerili Lesueur
Squatina squatina Linnaeus

SIZE: Normally 2 to 3 feet long, may reach 5 feet.

COLOR: Brown to gray-brown, lighter beneath.

RANGE: Florida to Long Island, occasionally to Cape Cod.

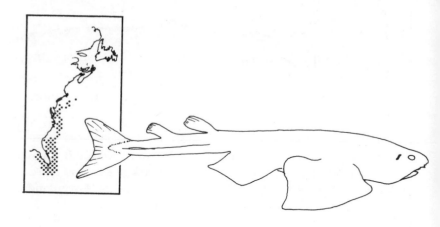

The angel shark looks like a cross between a skate and a shark. Its eyes are situated on top of a broad, rounded head. It has large, winglike pectoral fins and two small dorsal fins. The lower lobe of the caudal fin is longer than the upper. Angel sharks feed on a variety of bottom-dwelling marine animals but are themselves of little food value.

TORPEDOES, SKATES, AND RAYS — ORDER
Rajiformes (Batoidei, Hypotremata)

These unique fishes all have large, muscular pectoral fins, giving them a disklike or almost square appearance.

TORPEDOES (ELECTRIC RAYS) — FAMILY *Torpedinidae*

Torpedoes or electric rays possess two electric organs in the anterior portion of the pectoral fins.

This family of rays bears live young but there is no placental attachment between embryo and mother.

They are also known off the western European and African coasts.

Atlantic Torpedo
Electric ray, numbfish, crampfish, Atlantic torpedo
Torpedo nobiliana Bonaparte

SIZE: Two to 4 feet long, 5-footers have been caught but are unusual.

COLOR: Dark brown, sometimes with a reddish or bluish hue, white underneath.

RANGE: Nova Scotia to North Carolina, strays as far south as Georgia.

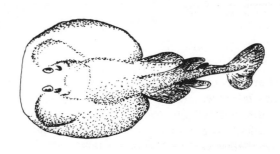

The torpedo is skatelike in appearance but somewhat fatter, softer, and smoother skinned. Its caudal fin is large and fishlike. The eyes are small, closely set, and close to the leading edge of the pectoral fins. The torpedo can impart a mild electric shock to an unwary fisherman, (although discharges in excess of 200 volts have been recorded from very large specimens.)

This is a bottom-dwelling fish subsisting on small fishes, typically flounder and other bottom fish.

Torpedoes breed in the warmer parts of their range and bear living young.

SKATES — FAMILY *Rajidae*

Skates are a bottom-feeding fish. Many species are so similar in appearance that most people have difficulty telling them apart.

Skates do not have the spine on the tail characteristic of the rays. They lay rectangular-shaped eggs with filaments at each corner. The empty egg cases found on the beach are often called "mermaids' purses," like the egg cases of certain dogfishes.

Most fishermen consider these fish a nuisance though many are excellent eating, and some species are highly regarded as food in Europe. Commercially there is a market for them as fish meal or pet food.

Unlike sharks, skates have 5 pairs of gill clefts located on the ventral surface. Skates and rays have round gill openings behind the eyes, but skates lack anal fins.

Barndoor skate
Sharpnose skate
Raja laevis Mitchill

SIZE: Usually 2½ to 4 feet long, occasionally reaching 5 feet.

COLOR: Brown to red-brown with dark blotches of varying sizes, light marbling and a distinct blotch on the trailing edge of each pectoral fin (may be absent), with the lower surface white to gray-white and spotted or streaked.

RANGE: North Carolina north to the Maritimes.

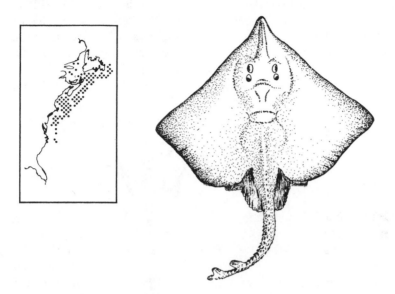

    This is our largest skate. Its pointed snout and the smooth skin on the pectoral fins clearly identify it. There are some spines at the base of the tail and on the tail.

    The barndoor skate is a bottom-feeder. It is found from the tide line to water over 100 fathoms deep.

    The barndoor skate is known to enter brackish waters.

Winter skate
Spotted skate, big skate, eyed skate
Raja ocellata Mitchill
Raja diaphanes Mitchill

SIZE: Commonly 2½ to 3 feet, occasionally 3½ feet long.

COLOR: Light brown with round dark spots above, a distinct eyed spot on the dorsal, posterior surface of the pectoral fin (a few specimens have lacked these spots). On each side of the snout ahead of the eyes is a translucent area. White undersides.

RANGE: Nova Scotia to North Carolina, strays somewhat north and south of these boundaries.

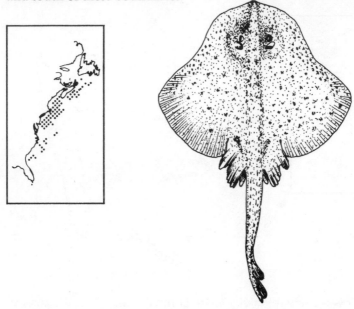

The clear area on each side of the snout, numerous spines, and a heavily toothed mouth are the best field marks of the big skate.

It is sometimes confused with the little skate (*R. erinacea,* page 59) but is somewhat larger and has more teeth. Along the coast the big skate is found in the winter months in water close to freezing. The little skate prefers warmer temperatures.

The big skate feeds on crabs, squid, and small fishes.

Clearnose skate
Rough skate, briar skate
Raja eglanteria Bosc

COLOR: Brown-gray above with dark spots and bars on the pectoral fins, white on the underside.

SIZE: Commonly 2 feet, may reach as much as 3 feet in length.

RANGE: Nova Scotia to Florida.

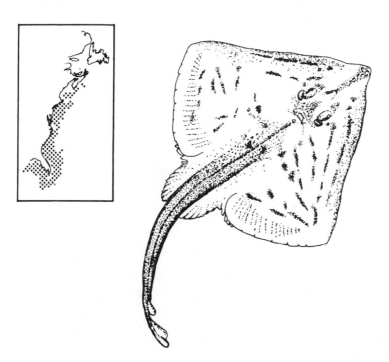

This big skate is primarily a southern fish, but can be expected to wander north of Cape Cod in late summer. It is a much smoother skate than the thorny skate with which it is sometimes confused.

Little skate
Common skate, summer skate
Raja erinacea Mitchill

SIZE: Most specimens are 16 to 18 inches long, they do not vary much in size.

COLOR: Gray, gray-brown, sometimes pinkish above, white or off-white below.

RANGE: Nova Scotia to Georgia.

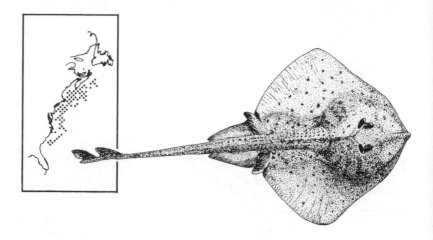

The little skate is a shoal-water species not usually found in water over 50 fathoms. It is our most common skate. Surf casters regularly curse these small skates, as they frequently grab the bait meant for striped bass.

The female has small thorns spread well over her body; the male has thorns along the front edge of the pectoral fins and down the tail only. It is rare to find spines on the centerline of the back or tail. A large specimen may closely resemble a big skate (*R. ocellata*), but it lacks both the eye spots and the translucent areas on each side of the snout.

Rosette skate
Leopard skate, spotted skate
Raja garmani Whitley

SIZE: Normally 1½ to 2 feet long.

COLOR: Light brown or pink-brown with many small dark spots and light blotches, rose-shaped clusters of dark spots and white to cream on the under surface.

RANGE: Florida to Cape Cod.

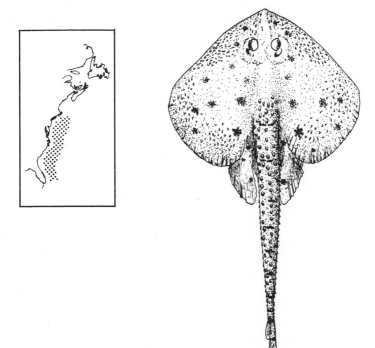

The rosette skate is an offshore fish rarely encountered in less than 25 fathoms of water. It frequents the waters off southern New England. It is plentiful south of Nantucket and occasionally a nuisance to fishermen in that area.

Smooth skate
Prickly skate, briar skate
Raja senta Garman

SIZE: Adults are consistently just under 2 feet long.

COLOR: Light gray-brown or tan with numerous darkish spots above; white, occasionally with a few blotches, dusky beneath.

RANGE: Nova Scotia to North Carolina.

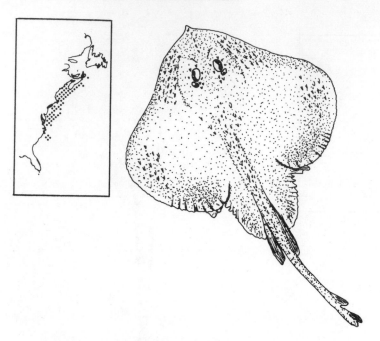

The smooth skate has a distinct row of thorns down the middle of its back and tail, as well as many small spines over most of its dorsal surface.

This is a deep-water species rarely occurring in less than 40 fathoms of water. It is most commonly encountered by commercial fishermen trawling on the fishing banks.

Thorny skate
Rough skate, starry skate
Raja radiata Donovan
Raja scabrata Garman

SIZE: Two to 3 feet long.

COLOR: Medium brown to gray-brown, modestly spotted above; white, sometimes with pale blotches, beneath.

RANGE: From the northernmost part of our range southward to Long Island, and straying as far south as Virginia.

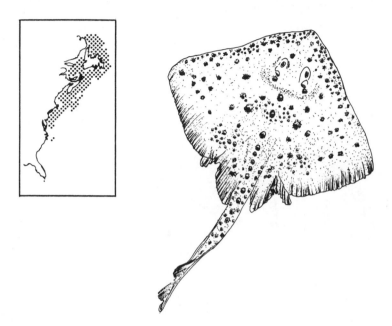

The thorny skate feeds on bottom-dwelling animals in the deeper, colder waters of our range. It is rarely seen close to shore.

There is a row of large thorns down the center of the back and tail, as well as 4 or 5 thorns spaced more or less evenly around the middle of the back.

Thorny skates eat a variety of marine animals, including shrimp, crabs, anemones, and fish.

STINGRAYS — FAMILY *Dasyatidae*

Stingrays may be distinguished from skates by a spine on the top of the base of the tail, which can cause a very painful injury, and somewhat more prominent teeth than the skates.

Roughtail stingray

Stingray, whiptail stingray, northern stingray, stingaree.
Dasyatis centroura Mitchill

SIZE: Known to exceed 10 feet in length and 5 feet in width.

COLOR: Dark brown above, tail nearly black, white underneath.

RANGE: Cape Cod to Georgia.

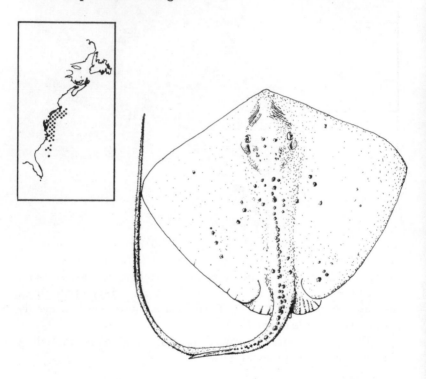

These stingrays can be distinguished from all other rays by the convex outline of the trailing edge of the pectoral fins, and the sharp angle between the leading and trailing edges. The stingray has a long, whiplike tail on which is a long, distinct spine. *D. centroura* is easily the largest of the northerly ranging stingrays.

Atlantic stingray
Stingaree ray, little stingray
Dasyatis sabina Lesueur

SIZE: Averages 3 to 3½ feet long.

COLOR: Dark brown above, white beneath.

RANGE: From Delaware south.

 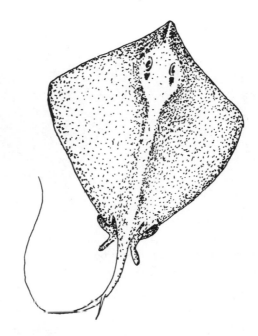

This is a small ray with rounded pectoral fins. It possesses a small spine on its tail capable of inflicting a painful wound if carelessly handled.

Smooth butterfly ray
Butterfly ray, lesser butterfly ray
Gymnura micrura Bloch and Schneider
Pteroplatea micrura Bloch and Schneider

SIZE: Occasionally exceeds 2 feet in width.

COLOR: Dark, reticulated pattern above, white below.

RANGE: Cape Cod and south; common in Florida waters.

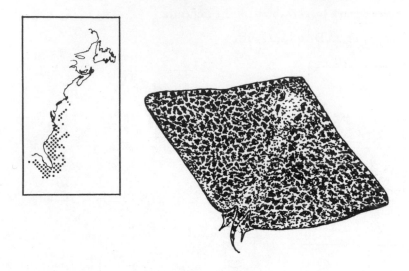

The butterfly ray is the only ray in our range with a tail shorter than its body. It is a bottom-feeder. It usually bears 2 live young.

EAGLE RAYS — FAMILY *Myliobatidae*

Eagle rays have bulging eyes, a long whiplike tail, and a single dorsal fin at the base of the tail.

Cownose ray
Rhinoptera bonasus Mitchill
Rhinoptera quadriloba Lesueur

SIZE: To 7 feet wide, more commonly half that size.

COLOR: Brown above, white to cream beneath; may have radiating lines on its back.

RANGE: Cape Cod and south, preferring the warmer seas.

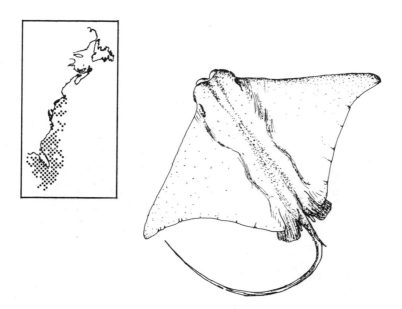

The cownose ray and its close relatives, unlike skates and stingrays, have their eyes on the sides of their head. They possess one, sometimes two spines at the base of the tail. They have been known to travel in sizable schools.

Their large, platelike teeth are enough to distinguish them from all other skates and rays in our range.

Bullnose ray
Eagle ray
Myliobatis freminvillei Lesueur

SIZE: To 5 feet wide.

COLOR: Plain grayish brown, lacking spots.

RANGE: From Cape Cod south.

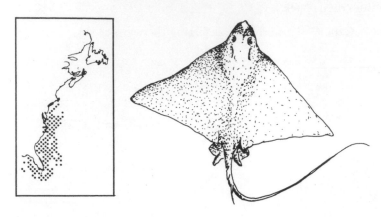

This eagle ray is a plain-colored ray well equipped with small teeth. It subsists mainly on various shellfish. Eagle rays bear live young.

Spotted eagle ray
Spotted whip ray
Aetobatus narinari Euphrasen

SIZE: Recorded to reach 12 feet in length.

COLOR: Numerous small light spots on the dorsal surface.

RANGE: Virginia and south.

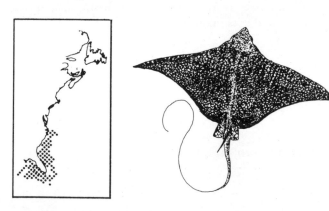

The spotted eagle ray is fairly scarce in our range. It is a bottom-feeder living on shellfish. It usually bears 4 live young.

DEVIL RAYS (MANTAS) — FAMILY *Mobulidae*

Devil rays or mantas differ from stingrays and cownosed rays by the earlike extensions curving forward at each side of the head, as well as by the greater sizes to which they grow.

Atlantic manta
Giant devil ray, manta, manta ray
Manta birostris Walbaum

SIZE: Recorded to have a "wingspread" of up to 22 feet.

COLOR: Red-brown, green-brown, or blue-brown above, occasionally with a few light blotches; white beneath.

RANGE: Occasionally seen offshore from Cape Cod, common from Virginia southward.

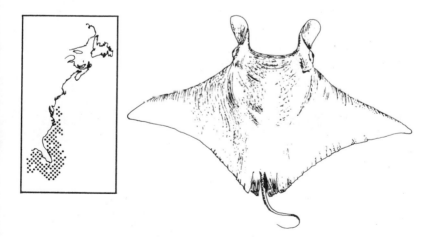

The Atlantic manta is a docile species presenting no threat to man in spite of its awesome appearance (although large rays may occasionally upset a small craft by accident) . It is known for its long leaps through the air, resembling a giant bat.

This massive ray is easily recognizable by the fleshy extensions of the pectoral fins, which project forward on either side of its extremely wide mouth.

Small mantas are an acceptable table fish, and larger specimens are sometimes utilized as pet food or fertilizer.

Mantas feed on small pelagic animals that are sifted out by their sievelike gill arches.

BONY FISHES*
CLASS *Osteichthyes* (Pisces)

The members of this class, regarded by some as the "true fishes," may be distinguished by a skeleton of true bone.[4] Most of them possess an air bladder, erectile fins with spines (rays), bony operculae (gill covers), and scales.

ORDER *Chondrostei* (Acipenseriformes)

STURGEONS — FAMILY *Acipenseridae*

There are two marine members of this family found in our range: the Atlantic sturgeon (*A. oxyrhynchus*) and the shortnose sturgeon (*A. brevirostrum*). They are both characterized by five rows of bony plates running the length of the body, by a spiracle between the eyes and the gill covers, and by a lack of teeth. The mouth is protuberant and placed well underneath to facilitate bottom feeding. These fishes usually have four barbels.

* Referred to as "true fishes" in older texts.

The Atlantic sturgeon is known for its roe (caviar). At one time, because of its eggs and its succulent meat, it supported a sizable fishery, but its numbers are so reduced today that it is rarely sought after commercially in this country.

Sturgeons spend most of their life at sea but ascend coastal rivers to spawn.

Atlantic sturgeon
Sea sturgeon, common sturgeon
Acipenser oxyrhynchus Mitchill
Acipenser sturio Linnaeus

SIZE: Atlantic sturgeon up to 18 feet in length could be expected years ago; today a specimen more than 9 feet long is unusual.

COLOR: Olive-gray or blue-gray above; lighter on the sides; white abdomen.

RANGE: Found in coastal waters and streams from the St. Lawrence River to South Carolina; stragglers reported southward to the Florida coast.

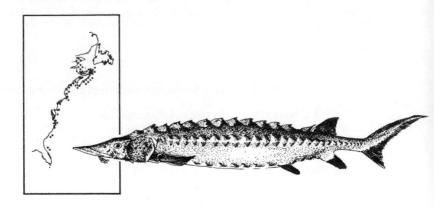

The Atlantic sturgeon is a slender fish with five longitudinal rows of bony plates. It has a long, pointed snout that is flat on the ventral surface. Its toothless mouth is placed totally on the ventral surface, slightly posterior to the eyes. The dorsal, ventral, and anal fins are placed well back on the body, and it has a heterocercal caudal fin.

The sturgeon ascends freshwater rivers to spawn in the late spring. The spent female, called a "cow," returns to the ocean in the fall. As many as 2½ million eggs may be deposited by a single female. The eggs hatch in about a week. The young sturgeon descend the river and some may remain in the lower reaches for several years before going to sea. Others, only a few inches long, called "sperlets," may go to sea their first year.

Sturgeons live on bottom-dwelling marine life such as worms and clams, and sometimes small fishes.

There has been a distinct decline in the number of sturgeons in our area, though recent efforts to clean up the rivers seems to be having a positive effect on the sturgeon population.

The sturgeon is of value as a meat fish and for its widely heralded roe, or "caviar."

Shortnose sturgeon
Little sturgeon
Acipenser brevirostrum Lesueur

SIZE: Specimens over 4 feet in length are uncommon.

COLOR: Black or dark gray on the back, light and dark alternating bands on the sides. May show a reddish hue, white abdomen.

RANGE: Mainly from Cape Cod to Florida; known in some coastal rivers of Maine.

The shortnose sturgeon closely resembles the Atlantic sturgeon but can be distinguished from it by the space between the dorsal shields, whereas in the Atlantic sturgeon these shields are in contact or overlapping. As its name implies, the shortnose sturgeon has a shorter, more rounded snout than a small Atlantic sturgeon.

The spawning habits of the shortnose sturgeon are typically anadromous: it spawns in freshwater streams and the young descend to the estuaries and migrate to the ocean as adults.

The shortnose sturgeon is too uncommon on our coast to have any commercial importance.

ORDER *Elopiformes*

TARPONS — FAMILY *Elopidae*

Ladyfish
Ten-pounder
Elops saurus Linnaeus

SIZE: To 3 feet, but commonly less than 2 feet in length.

COLOR: Silver back and sides; belly and fins yellow-gold to yellow-gray.

RANGE: Mainly Florida to North Carolina; may reach Cape Cod in the summer.

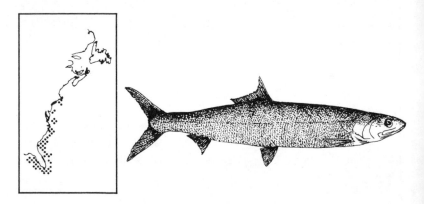

The ladyfish has noticeably smaller scales than the tarpon or herrings, with which it might be confused. The dorsal fin has a concave outline but lacks the threadlike ray of the tarpon's dorsal fin.

Because of its preference for the shallow waters of bights and estuaries, the ladyfish is eagerly sought after by anglers using light saltwater tackle. It is a good food fish, but rather bony.

Tarpon
Sabelo
Megalops atlantica Cuvier and Valenciennes
Tarpon atlanticus Cuvier and Valenciennes

SIZE: Known to exceed 8 feet in length.

COLOR: Bright silver all over, with a deep blue-green iridescence on the back.

RANGE: A southern fish ranging to Long Island and occasionally to Cape Cod; may round the Cape in the summer.

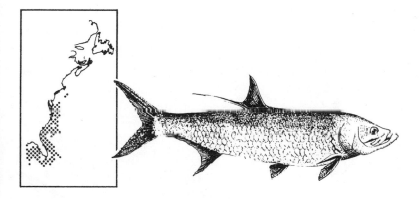

Only a very small tarpon could be confused with any other species. Its proportionately large scales and threadlike ray on the trailing edge of the dorsal fin should clearly distinguish it.

A true sporting fish, the tarpon is a popular quarry with fishermen not only because of its size but also because of the spectacular leaps it makes when hooked. (Most tarpon fishermen carefully release their catch since tarpon are not considered an acceptable food fish.)

Tarpon are primarily warm water fish, and are not able to tolerate water much below 65° F. They prefer shallow waters. At night or in the early morning hours, they feed in the shallows on crustaceans, mullet, and other small fishes.

In the summer the female tarpon lays eggs which hatch into transparent larvae. The young live on plankton until they are several inches long.

BONEFISHES — FAMILY *Albulidae*

Bonefish
Ladyfish
Albula vulpes Linnaeus

SIZE: Rarely exceeds 30 inches.

COLOR: Blue-gray to green-gray with dark cross bands on the back; white or cream beneath; silvery cast on the sides.

RANGE: Mainly from Florida to New Jersey, rarely to Cape Cod. Far more common in tropical seas.

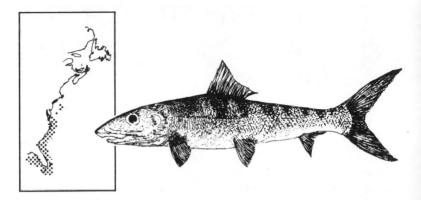

The only member of the Family Albulidae in our range. The bonefish is tubular in shape, with a large mouth placed well beneath the head. It has small scales and a deeply forked caudal fin. A close relative, the longfin bonefish (*Dixonina nemoptera*), inhabits more tropical waters.

Though the bonefish has no food value, its erratic and unpredictable behavior makes it very hard to catch, and it is therefore considered one of the most challenging game fishes in our range. It makes incredibly long, fast runs once it has been hooked.

EELS — ORDER *Anguilliformes* (Apodes)

These snakelike, scaleless or tiny-scaled fishes are not likely to be confused with any other species in our area. They have continuous dorsal, caudal, and anal fins, and lack a ventral fin.

FRESHWATER EELS
(TRUE EELS) — FAMILY *Anguillidae*

American eel
Eel, true eel, freshwater eel, elver (young form) , common eel
Anguilla rostrata Lesueur

SIZE: Reaches 4 to 5 feet in length.

COLOR: Olive-brown, dark brown to black above; yellowish sides; yellow-brown to cream white beneath.

RANGE: Nova Scotia and southward.

The American eel is distinguishable by its continuous dorsal, caudal, and anal fins, originating well behind the gill slit, its small pectorals just above the gill slits, and a lower jaw extending beyond the upper. Its eyes are small and placed well forward on the head, wholly over the mouth.

The life history of the American eel remained a mystery for many years, until finally, in 1922, after 18 years of searching, the Danish scientist Johannes Schmidt discovered that the ripe female eels travel thousands of miles to the Sargasso Sea to spawn. The hatchlings, called "leptocephali," make the reverse journey to the coastal streams of northern Europe, as well as North America, where their parents originated. By the time the young eels have reached the rivers they have grown into "elvers" and closely resemble adults but are only a few inches long. The females then ascend the rivers far upstream, sometimes by underground waterways, sometimes appearing mysteriously in ponds with no visible connection to the sea. After several years they descend back to the sea to return to their traditional spawning grounds to lay their eggs and then die.

Eels have long been a popular table fish in Europe. In the United States they are far less popular, except perhaps for families of European background.

CONGER EELS — FAMILY *Congridae*

Conger eel
American conger, sea eel
Conger oceanicus (*oceanus*) Mitchill
Leptocephalus conger Linnaeus

SIZE: Usually from 3 to 5 feet in length, but known to exceed 15 feet.

COLOR: Brown-gray or blue-gray to black above; sides lighter, sometimes with a coppery tinge; dull white beneath.

RANGE: Throughout our range. Large conger eels are not common north of Cape Cod.

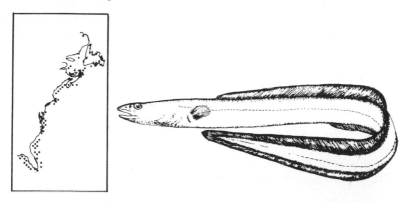

The conger is a scaleless, wholly marine eel. It is heavier bodied than the American eel. Its dorsal, caudal, and anal fins are continuous, as in the American eel, but start just behind the pectoral fin. Its upper jaw is slightly longer than the lower, and the eyes are large and extend slightly behind the mouth.

The conger eel prefers waters near the shore, but retreats to deep water to spawn.

HERRINGLIKE FISHES — ORDER
Clupeiformes (Isospondyli)

This order contains a large variety of fishes with soft, rayed fins. Their dorsal fin is placed well back; the ventral fins are beneath or posterior to the dorsal, while the caudal fin is deeply forked. An adipose (soft, fleshy, and rayless) fin is present in the smelt, trout, and salmon families.

Several members of this order ascend rivers from the sea to breed, and some, while being primarily freshwater species, winter at sea. The herrings and their relatives are among the most commercially important of all the world's major food fishes.

TRUE HERRINGS — FAMILY *Clupeidae*

This is a large family of small, silvery fishes that lack a lateral line, are without an adipose fin, and usually have a deeply forked caudal fin and small or no teeth. Some species, *C. harengus* in particular, support major fisheries. Many members of this family are so similar that all are usually referred to simply as "herring" on the market.

Atlantic herring
Sea herring, common herring, Labrador sardine, sardine (young), sperling, brit
Clupea harengus Linnaeus
Clupea harengus harengus Linnaeus

SIZE: Reaches a length of 18 inches but averages less than 12 inches.

COLOR: Deep gray-blue to green-blue on the back; sides and belly silver; may have a green-gray band running lengthwise and low on its sides.

RANGE: From the northernmost part of our range south to Nantucket and, in winter, to south of Long Island.

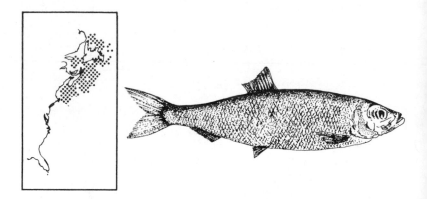

The Atlantic herring is a laterally flattened fish. The dorsal fin originates about the halfway point of the body. In other herrings it is situated somewhat more forward. The Atlantic herring has large, loose scales and a slightly serrated abdominal edge. It is distinguishable from other herrings by its toothed vomer—that is, it has teeth in the middle of the roof of the mouth—and by its comparatively shallow abdomen.

C. harengus travels in vast schools in the open ocean in water averaging 38° to 40° F in temperature. It is not found in tropical or subtropical waters.

Spawning takes place in the fall and the fry may reach a length of 5 inches in a year. The fry, as well as the adults, subsist primarily on planktonic sea life.

The commercial fisheries for the sea herring rank among the most important in the world; annual catches have exceeded 75,000 tons in a year in our range alone. Young herring are packed as "sardines"; adults are eaten fresh, salted, smoked, or pickled.

Round herring
Etrumeus teres DeKay
Etrumeus sadina Mitchill

SIZE: Rarely exceeds 10 inches.

COLOR: Bright green-gray back, silver on sides and beneath; color and brilliance fade rapidly at death.

RANGE: North primarily to Long Island, occasionally to Cape Cod, which it rounds but rarely.

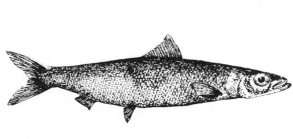

This fish is easily identified by its tubular-shaped body and long, pointed head. Its abdomen does not come to a sharp edge, like that of other herrings. Its dorsal fin originates well ahead of the ventrals. It is distinguished from the ladyfish by much larger scales.

Hickory shad
Fall herring, shad herring, shad
Alosa mediocris Mitchill
Pomolobus mediocris Mitchill

SIZE: Reaches 2 feet in length.

COLOR: Green-gray above, silvery sides and belly, faint longitudinal stripes on upper half of body; adults have a short row of dark spots directly behind the gills.

RANGE: Throughout our range, more populous south of Cape Cod.

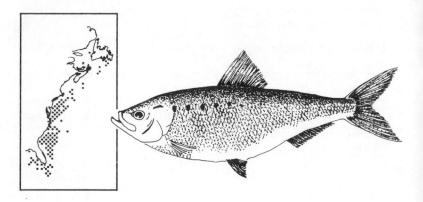

This is the second largest herring in our range (the American shad, *A. sapidissima*, see below, is slightly larger). It has a rather flat back and deep belly. Its mouth opens upward, the lower jaw extending well beyond the upper. The hickory shad is anadromous and rarely ventures very far to sea. It is a fine sports fish and is sought commercially as well.

The hickory shad subsists more on small fish than other herrings do.

Gizzard shad
Dorosoma cepedianum Lesueur

SIZE: To 15 inches, 10 inches common.

COLOR: Dark greenish above, silvery sides, near white beneath.

RANGE: Cape Cod and southward, common from North Carolina to Florida and the Gulf of Mexico.

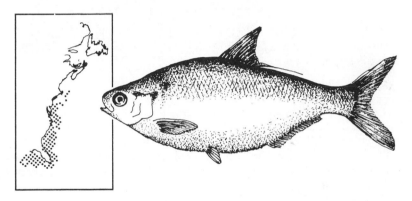

The gizzard shad is a brackish- and freshwater herring. It may be identified by the threadlike ray on its dorsal fin. It has no lateral line and no teeth, and has bony serratures on the abdomen. Gizzard shad differ in habits from other herrings in that they obtain their food from muddy bottoms, straining out small organisms by means of gill rakers.

The gizzard shad has no commercial value but it is an important forage food for predatory fishes.

American shad
Shad, common shad
Alosa sapidissima Wilson

SIZE: To 2½ feet, average length 18 to 20 inches.

COLOR: Dark blue, blue-green, or green above, light silver on sides and belly. A line of spots is usually present directly behind the gill covers, in line with the eyes and not extending beyond the dorsal fin.

RANGE: Nova Scotia to northern Florida.

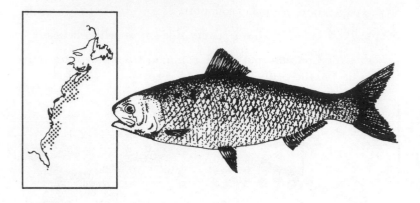

This is the largest herring in our range. It could easily be confused with other herrings except that its lower jaw closes entirely *within* the upper one, making the American shad readily identifiable. The jaw extends to the rear margin of the eye. As an adult the American shad totally lacks teeth.

The American shad ascend to spawn large rivers, where commercial fishermen net them. Their fine flesh and tasty roe make them popular with both sport and commercial fishermen. Extensive fishing has reduced their numbers in rivers such as the Potomac, where the hickory shad has pretty nearly taken over.

The shad spawns in the spring and the newly hatched shad remain in the river until fall, when they go to sea. From 2 to 5 years later they repeat the cycle.

Alewife
Graywife, freshwater herring, sawbelly, branch herring
Alosa pseudoharengus Wilson
Pomolobus pseudoharengus Wilson

SIZE: Reaches a length of 15 inches, but is commonly less than a foot long. Landlocked specimens rarely exceed 6 inches.

COLOR: Dark gray-green on the back; light sliver gray-green on the sides and belly. A dark spot is usually present directly behind the gills, in line with the eyes.

RANGE: Common only from Nova Scotia to North Carolina, though known from Labrador to Florida.

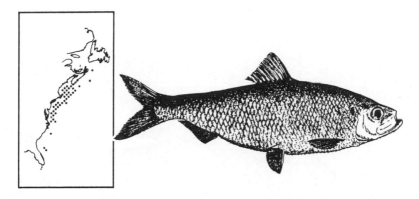

The alewife can be distinguished from the Atlantic herring (*C. harengus*) by the deep, sawtooth outline of the belly, and by a dorsal fin that starts distinctly forward of the middle of the fish. It may be distinguished from the blueback (*P. aestivalis*, see below) by its eye, which is of greater diameter than the distance from the eye to the tip of the snout.

Alewives are strongly anadromous, ascending freshwater streams in great numbers in the spring to spawn in ponds. The female lays as many as 100,000 or more eggs.

Commercially, alewives are netted out of the spawning runs in great numbers. They are canned, smoked, salted, or sold as bait.

Alewives also have become landlocked. In fresh water they are apparently vulnerable to rapid temperature changes, which seem to be the cause of the mass mortalities that frequently occur among them in the summer.

Blueback herring
Glut herring, summer herring, kyack
Alosa aestivalis Mitchill
Pomolobus aestivalis Mitchill

SIZE: Reaches 15 inches in length, but averages 12 inches.

COLOR: Blue to blue-gray above, silver sides and belly sometimes with a reddish tinge; first few rows of scales spotted, giving the appearance of longitudinal stripes.

RANGE: Nova Scotia to Florida.

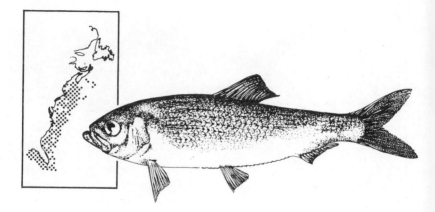

The blueback and alewife (*P. pseudoharengus*) closely resemble one another, except that the eye of the blueback is equal in diameter to the distance from the eye to the snout, and the eye of the alewife is proportionately larger. An interior characteristic is the black lining of the intestines of the blueback, whereas the lining is gray or pink in the alewife.

Bluebacks spend most of their lives in salt water but run up freshwater streams to spawn, seeming to prefer the smaller tributaries. The fry return to sea, as do the spent females, sooner than do most other herrings. Little is known of their habits at sea except that like many other herrings, they travel in large schools. They are a popular bait fish but are commercially important only as an incidental catch.

Atlantic menhaden
Menhaden, pogy, fatback, mossbunker
Brevoortia tyrannus Latrobe

SIZE: Averages 15 inches in length, 2- and 3-inch individuals school in large numbers in channels, inlets, and estuaries in the summer.

COLOR: Dark blue or blue-brown above; sides and belly silver, often with a yellow tinge. A conspicuous spot is usually present directly behind the gill covers at eye level.

RANGE: Nova Scotia to Florida.

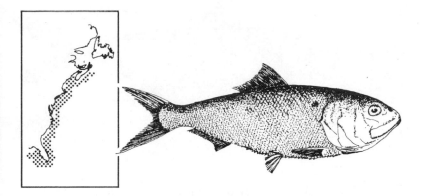

This member of the herring tribe is an important source of oil, fish meal, and pet food.

It can be identified by its large, scaleless head, straight-margined scales, small ventral fins, and toothless mouth.

Because of its unusually large numbers and its habit of traveling in immense, tightly packed schools, the Atlantic menhaden is an important source of food for other fish. Its migrations often are a key to the movements of many of the larger fishes such as bluefish, striped bass, and various tunas.

Menhaden feed on diatoms and very small crustaceans as well as small worms, unicellular plants, and a variety of other very small plant and animal life.

Atlantic thread herring
Thread herring
Opisthonema oglinum Lesueur

SIZE: Reaches 12 inches in length.

COLOR: Bluish on the back, silver on sides and belly; first few rows of scales spotted, giving the appearance of stripes.

RANGE: Chesapeake Bay and south, rarely north to Cape Cod.

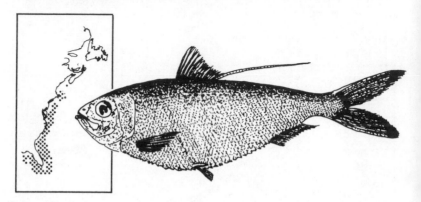

This herring can easily be identified by the long, threadlike last ray of its dorsal fin. Its deep belly is strongly sawtoothed. The Atlantic thread herring is primarily a tropical fish and never abundant in temperate waters. Where it does occur, its small size makes it a popular source of food for many predatory species.

Spanish sardine
Spanish herring, anchovy
Sardinella anchovia Cuvier and Valenciennes

SIZE: To 6 inches long, usually somewhat smaller.

COLOR: Translucent silver with a faint, thin band running from the gill to the caudal fin.

RANGE: From Cape Cod southward, considerably more populous in southern waters.

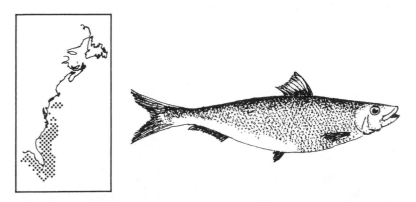

The Spanish sardine prefers tropical waters and is seldom seen in large numbers far north of Florida. It is mentioned here because in recent years it has been sought after by the fishing industry and on occasion appears in significant numbers within our range.

It feeds on plankton, copepods, and other small marine life.

ANCHOVIES — FAMILY *Engraulidae*

These small, silvery fishes are characterized by a wide, under-slung mouth and large eyes. A number of these typically tropical species frequently stray into our range.

Bay anchovy
Anchovy whitebait, common anchovy
Anchoa mitchilli Cuvier and Valenciennes

SIZE: To 4 inches long.

COLOR: Translucent silver with a faint, narrow band running from gills to caudal fin; small dark specks irregularly placed over the body.

RANGE: Maine and southward; not common north of Cape Cod.

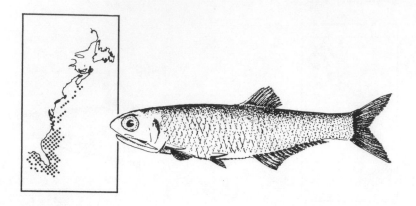

This little fish can be distinguished by its proportionately outsized eyes and large loose scales. Its dorsal fin originates well back, almost entirely over the anal fin, and the pectoral and ventral fins are located very low (abdominally). The tail fin is deeply forked. The mouth is large and wholly ventral. The fish lacks an adipose fin.

Common anchovies support a major commercial fishery and are marketed in the form of the familiar "anchovy paste."

Striped anchovy
Anchoa hepsetus Linnaeus
Anchoviella hepsetus Bonnaterre
Stolephorus brownii Jordan and Evermann

SIZE: Reaches 6 inches in length, more commonly less than 5 inches.

COLOR: Light gray-green with yellowish tinges above, often with some dark spots; a bright silver stripe from gills to caudal fin; light silver beneath.

RANGE: Mainly from Maryland south, straying as far north as the Gulf of Maine.

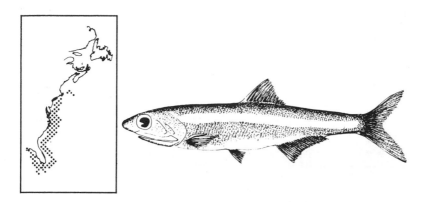

This is the largest anchovy in our area. Its single dorsal fin distinguishes it from the silversides and its lack of an adipose fin differentiates it from the smelts. It differs from the other anchovies in that its anal fin originates beneath the last few rays of the dorsal fin. The mouth is large and wholly ventral. The tail is deeply forked.

The striped anchovy travels in large schools and feeds on small or microscopic marine animals. In turn, it is preyed upon by a variety of larger fishes.

It is a commercially valuable fish when sufficient numbers can be found. It is marketed pickled or salted.

Silver anchovy
Anchoviella argyrophanus Cuvier and Valenciennes

SIZE: Rarely exceeds 6 inches in length.

COLOR: Bright silver, slightly darker on the back.

RANGE: Frequently wanders into the southern part of our range.

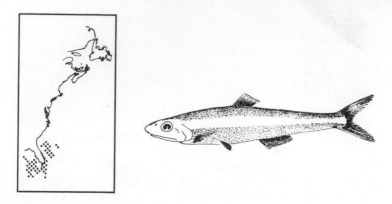

The silver anchovy is distinguished from the striped by the anal fin, which originates wholly behind the dorsal. It is also slimmer than the striped anchovy.

The young hatch from small, elliptical eggs, which float in the open sea.

ORDER *Salmoniformes*

TROUTS AND SALMONS — FAMILY *Salmonidae*[5]

This attractive family of soft-rayed fishes is made up of some of our most desirable sports fish. They excel in their challenge to the sportsman and are a favorite among gourmets for their fine flavor.

Trouts and salmons are characterized by an adipose fin, small cycloid scales (all but the largest members of the family appear scaleless), and pelvic fins that originate farther back than does the dorsal fin.

Salmons are anadromous; that is, they leave the sea each spring to ascend the coastal streams to spawn, each to the river of its origin, fighting against seemingly hopeless odds through waterfalls, rapids, fallen trees, and so on. So exhausted are they when they reach their spawning pool that after laying and fertilizing the eggs, they soon die. (The Atlantic salmon is an exception. It may survive to return to sea.)

Economically, trouts and salmons are significant. Considerable funds are spent each year to transplant fry, support hatcheries, and stock rivers and lakes. Considerable time and money are spent on reclaiming ponds and streams, making them again suitable for these fish by cleaning them up and getting rid of undesirable species living in them.

Rainbow trout are by far the most successful hatchery fish, brown trout less so. Brook trout are an experimental hatchery fish and some success has been achieved in increasing their numbers by planting fertile eggs in stream beds.

The Atlantic salmon is the only truly native salmon in our area and supports a major commercial fishery. These fish are gill-netted at the mouths of rivers and trawled for in the open sea. Sports fishermen seek the Atlantic salmon with equal enthusiasm, coming from many parts of the world to fish the famous salmon rivers of North America and northern Europe. Sockeye, humpback or pink salmon ("kokanee" when landlocked), and coho salmon have been introduced from the West Coast into a number of rivers and lakes in the northeastern United States, as well as the Great Lakes, with varying degrees of success.

Atlantic salmon
Sea salmon, silver salmon, ouananiche
Salmo salar Linnaeus

SIZE: Atlantic salmon about 30 inches long and weighing from 15 to 20 pounds are to be expected, but the species grows to trophy proportions of over 70 pounds.

COLOR: Generally silver above and below, with a blue-black hue on the dorsal surface; upper half of the body has small X-shaped spots. Young salmon are variously colored, being similar to trout in appearance.

RANGE: Spawns in coastal rivers in the northeastern United

States, Canada, and Greenland; is found in offshore waters off
the southern coasts of the Maritimes and Greenland.

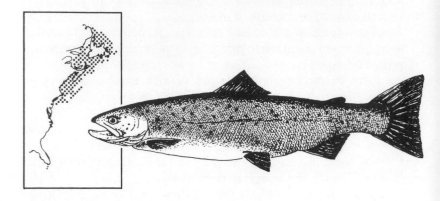

Usually in the spring (some salmon start upstream in the
summer, a few as late as mid-autumn), large, robust, silvery sea
salmon enter the rivers of their birth to spawn. Strong instinct
drives these handsome fish far upstream, overcoming seemingly
insurmountable obstacles such as rapids, rocks, falls, and dams.
They eat little or nothing along the way and by the time they
reach the spawning grounds they are weak and emaciated. The
male develops a strongly hooked lower jaw, which meet at the tips
only, and is called a "kype." The female lays large, heavily shelled
eggs that are immediately fertilized by the male in a large "redd"
(a nest of pebbles prepared on the stream bed). The larvae,
called "alevin," carry a yolk sac for the first six or seven weeks
after hatching. Once the yolk sacs are absorbed, the young fish
slowly descend the river, driven by instinct each year toward the
sea. By this time they have developed a barred pattern very similar to that of the young brown trout (*S. trutta*) or brook trout
(*S. fontinalis*); salmon, however, have a more deeply forked tail
and a smaller mouth. These "parr" remain in the stream two to
three years (up to six years in some Norwegian rivers), slowly
changing to a silvery color. Finally these "smolt" enter the sea.
Once in the marine environment they feed voraciously on a variety of aquatic life, including insects and worms. Now known as

"grilse," they may return to the river they hatched in as year-lings. Those that remain at sea are called "true salmon" and may attain immense proportions, sometimes exceeding 70 pounds.

Unlike West Coast salmon, *S. salar* does not always die upon spawning, and some of these salmon may return a second or third time to spawn. Fish that survive the spawning run and return to sea are known as "kelts."

Brown trout
Salter
Salmo trutta Linnaeus

SIZE: Can exceed 2 feet in length and 18 pounds in weight; specimens of 40 pounds have been recorded.

COLOR: Brownish with large, dark brown spots that may or may not be ringed in white, mixed with black spots on back and upper sides; haloed orange or red spots on sides. Loses most of its coloration after being at sea, becoming silvery like the Atlantic salmon (*S. salar*) grilse. The freshwater coloration returns when fish reenters the freshwater environment.

RANGE: Widely introduced in the northern half of our range.

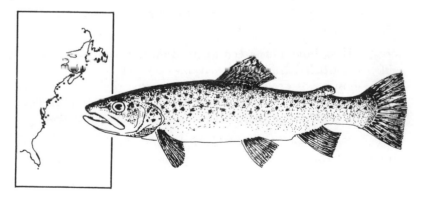

Brown trout are native European trout that were widely introduced into North America, starting in 1883, as well as other parts of the world.

Browns occasionally enter the marine environment, as do some other fishes that are normally found in fresh water. (Some strains of trout in Europe have apparently become anadromous and predictably go to sea after spawning.) In the United States brown trout appear to make random trips to the sea, or possibly they are forced downstream to the salt water because of crowding or a shortage of food. What research has been done shows that at sea their diet is quite varied, including shrimp, small fishes, and so on. They may be distinguished from salmon by the absence of the X-shaped spots, which are characteristic of salmon only. The brown trout is also clearly distinguishable from salmon, as well as from brook and rainbow trout, by the double row of well-developed teeth on the roof of its mouth (vomerine teeth). The dorsal fin has 10 to 13 rays, the anal fin 9 or 10. The tail fin varies from slightly forked to slightly rounded.

Large adult males develop the hooked jaws characteristic of male salmon.

Brook trout
Speckled trout, salter
Salvelinus fontinalis Mitchill

SIZE: Sea-run specimens may grow to over 15 inches; inland fish are somewhat smaller.

COLOR: Dark blue, blue-green to green on the back, silver on the side, white belly; freshwater markings include red spots on the sides, mostly obscured on sea-run specimens; dorsal and caudal fins are mottled. "Wild" or native trout have red or pink flesh, while hatchery fish usually have white or nearly white flesh.

RANGE: From Georgia north to Labrador. Range and populations are strongly influenced by local stocking programs.

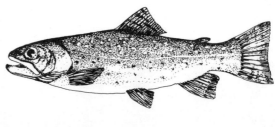

Occasionally these freshwater trout enter salt water, providing excellent sport when they return to the estuaries. Except for their lack of color and, often, their larger size, sea-run brook trout are identical to freshwater brookies.

Brook trout have well-developed teeth; the dorsal fin has 10 rays, the anal fin 9, and the caudal fin is slightly forked or square (hence the nickname "squaretail").

Rainbow trout
Steelhead (migratory form), salter
Salmo gairdneri Richardson
Salmo irideus Gibbons

SIZE: A 15-inch fish is common; sea-run steelheads weighing up to 36 pounds have been taken.

COLOR: Sea-runs are gray-blue above, with the upper half of the body spotted. Faint rosy band along lateral line; white belly; silvery tinge all over. Freshwater fish have deeper colors.

RANGE: From Nova Scotia to Florida, depending on regional stocking programs. (Transplanted from West Coast)

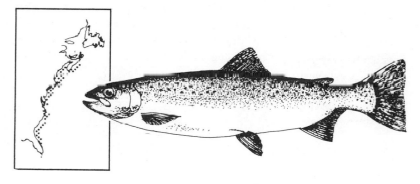

Rainbow trout, or steelheads, have a nearly square tail, and the dorsal and caudal fins are spotted. Rainbow trout are currently the most widely stocked fish in our area. Many sea-run rainbows are escapees from coastal trout hatcheries. Fish from hatcheries do not have the brilliant colors of native fish.

Rainbows exhibit a distinct anadromous instinct. Individuals have been tagged at spawning time, and the following year recovered in the same freshwater stream, to which they had again come to spawn.

SMELTS — FAMILIES *Osmeridae* and *Argentinidae*

The smelts are the smallest relatives of the salmons. They are easily distinguished from the young of their relatives by their pointed snouts and long, slim bodies.

Rainbow smelt
American smelt, Atlantic smelt, saltwater smelt, Arctic smelt, smelt
Osmerus mordax Mitchill

SIZE: To 14 inches long, more commonly 8 to 10 inches.

COLOR: Translucent green, green-olive to green-brown above (sea-run smelts are decidedly darker than landlocked smelts or those that have spent the greater part of their life in fresh water) ; sides and belly are silvery. A silvery band, sometimes quite indistinct runs from behind the gills at eye level to the caudal fin; this band is indistinct in large seagoing specimens, whose sides and belly are strongly silver.

RANGE: Mainly from Nova Scotia to New Jersey; occasionally strays well beyond these bounds.

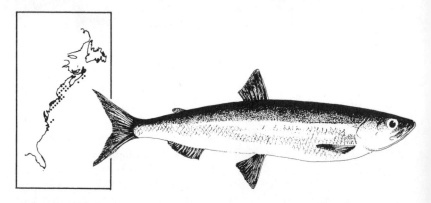

This small, anadromous member of the Argentinidae was once abundant at the mouths of rivers in its range at spawning time. Today, with careful maintenance and conservation, smelt populations still yield enough fish to support a commercial fishery, but their numbers are only a fraction of what they were a hundred years ago. Some states now have strict laws to control smelt fishing.

Smelt have large canine teeth on the roof of the mouth (vomer) and on the surface of the tongue.

The saltwater smelt rarely strays far from the coast. It feeds on shrimp, worms, and other small fish.

Despite their small size, smelt rank high on the list of sea foods. Ripe females yield delicious roe.

Capelin
Mallotus villosus Müller

SIZE: Rarely exceeds 7 inches in length.

COLOR: Translucent green to olive-brown above; silver sides; white belly.

RANGE: Frequents the northern part of our range, occasionally ranging as far south as Cape Cod.

The capelin is a small offshore fish which is seen in numbers near the shore during the breeding season. Capelin lay their eggs just below the low-water mark on Arctic and sub-Arctic shores. It is not uncommon to see large numbers of them thrown up on the shore by the surf.

The capelin is somewhat more slender than the smelt (*O. mordax*). The mouth extends to halfway behind the lower margin of the large eye; in the smelt it extends noticeably farther back, under a smaller eye.

These little fish are considered a delight on the table.

Atlantic argentine[6]
Herring smelt, argentine
Argentina silus Ascanius

SIZE: Attains a length of 10 inches.

COLOR: Brown or green-brown on the back, sides silver or brass.

RANGE: Nova Scotia to Long Island.

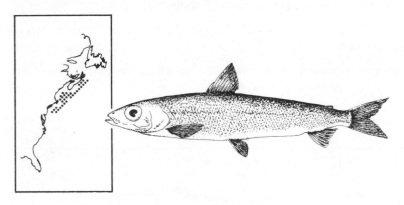

The argentine is the largest member of the smelt family. It can be distinguished from other Argentinidae by its small mouth, which is wholly *ahead* of the very large eye. Its dorsal fin is situated entirely ahead of the ventral fin.

These deep-water smelt are occasionally caught in trawls on the fishing banks. They breed in deep water but not a great deal is known about their diet or life history.

ORDER *Myctophiformes*

This order includes a number of unusual deep-water fish families that are not frequently encountered. It is represented here by the lancetfish.

LANCETFISHES — FAMILY *Alepisauridae*

Longnose lancetfish
Lancetfish
Alepisaurus ferox Lowe

SIZE: Ordinarily attains a length of about 3 feet; specimens up to 6 feet long have been recorded.

COLOR: Dark gray back, silver sides and belly.

RANGE: In deep water from Newfoundland to Long Island.

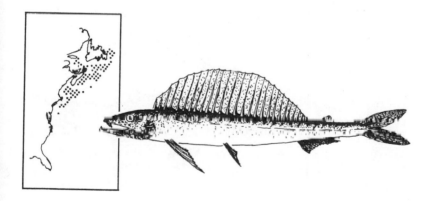

This is an offshore fish occasionally captured in nets on the traditional fishing grounds in our range.

Its long, slender body, long, high dorsal fin, and fanglike teeth clearly identify it. It is scaleless. There is not a great deal known about its life habits.

ORDER *Siluriformes* (Nematognathi)

SEA CATFISHES — FAMILY *Ariidae* (Siluridae)

This is a family of scaleless, moderately sized fish with conspicuous barbels. Of the three members of the family, two inhabit our area.

Sea catfish
Hard cat
Arius felis Linnaeus
Galeichthys felis Linnaeus

SIZE: Ordinarily reaches a length of about 1 foot; maximum length about 18 inches.

COLOR: Gray-blue to deep gray above, white or yellow-white below.

RANGE: Cape Cod and south, common from Virginia southward.

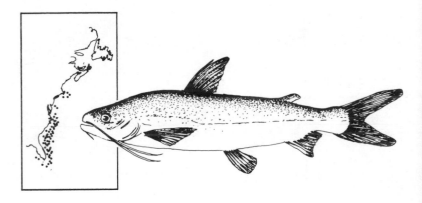

The hard thick first spine of the dorsal and pectoral fins, which can cause painful puncture wounds, an adipose fin, and two sets of barbels, one on the upper and the other on the lower jaw, are the chief distinguishing characteristics of the sea catfish.

It is easily caught by hook and line but it is not favored as a food fish.

The male sea catfish has the unusual habit of incubating the eggs and larvae in its mouth, during which period it does not eat.

Gafftopsail catfish
Whisker catfish
Bagre marinus Mitchill

SIZE: Reaches a length of 2 feet.

COLOR: Gray-blue above, silver below; dorsal, adipose, and caudal fins dusky and yellow-green.

RANGE: From Cape Cod south.

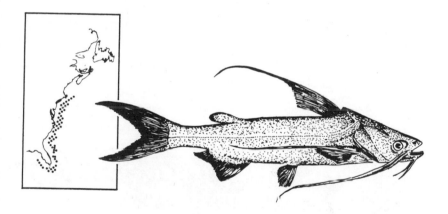

The extended rays of the dorsal and pectoral fins and the long barbels of the upper jaw distinguish the gafftopsail from the sea catfish (*A. felis*). As is typical of catfish, it has an adipose fin and lacks scales.

This is an excellent food fish but suffers because of the reputation of its close relative the sea catfish. It also ranks as a good sports fish.

The male gafftopsail, like the sea cat, incubates the eggs and larvae in its mouth.

ORDER *Lophiiformes* (Pediculati)

GOOSEFISHES — FAMILY *Lophiidae*

This is a small but unusual family of angler fishes with fleshy
pectoral fins and an enormous mouth. The goosefish is commonly encountered in our area.

Goosefish
American goosefish, angler, monkfish
Lophius americanus Cuvier and Valenciennes
Lophius piscatorius Linnaeus

SIZE: Reaches a length of 4 feet, usually somewhat smaller.

COLOR: Brown with mottling and spots, belly nearly white; pectoral, dorsal, and caudal fins dark edged.

RANGE: Throughout our range.

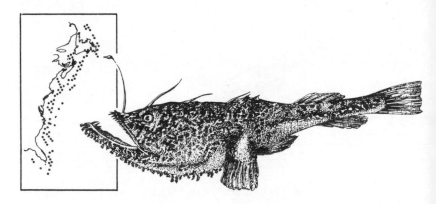

    The first dorsal fin is a modified spine with a small, fleshy
tip that dangles over the large, well-toothed mouth to attract
prey. Unsuspecting fish wandering too close are sucked in and
swallowed. The goosefish includes sea birds in its diet by capturing them in the shallows or grabbing diving birds such as
cormorants and grebes as these birds are searching for sub-
marine food.

In spite of its ungainly appearance, the goosefish has excellent-tasting flesh and is readily marketable.

The goosefish can be found all the way from the low-tide line to the continental slope.

FROGFISHES — FAMILY *Antennariidae*

Sargassumfish
Mouse fish, frog fish
Histrio histrio Linnaeus
Histrio pictus Cuvier and Valenciennes

SIZE: Rarely exceeds 6 inches in length.

COLOR: Cream colored with brown blotches and mottling overall; yellow tips on the fleshy appendages.

RANGE: Common off the Florida coast, drifting sporadically as far north as Cape Cod.

The sargassumfish uses its fleshy pectoral fins to climb about on drifting clumps of sargassum weed, looking for a tasty meal.

These fish are only occasionally found near shore. They drift
northward in clumps of seaweed from their more normal habitats in tropical and subtropical waters.

The armlike pectoral fins and soft, loose skin with fleshy
tabs clearly distinguish this fish from any other in our area.

ORDER *Batrachoidiformes* (Haplodoci)

TOADFISHES — FAMILY *Batrachoididae*

Oyster toadfish
Toadfish
Opsanus tau Linnaeus

SIZE: Averages 10 to 12 inches in length.

COLOR: Dark markings on brown-yellow or brown-green, in the
form of irregular bars and blotches. Coloration varies with habitat.

RANGE: A southern species ranging normally to Cape Cod, strays
wandering as far north as Nova Scotia.

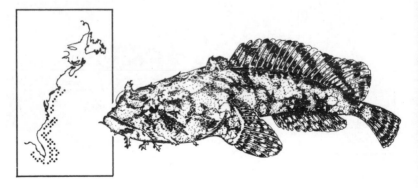

A large head, gaping mouth, fleshy appendages about the
head, and ventral fins ahead of the pectorals are identifying
characteristics of the toadfish.

The toadfish is a hardy fish capable of living out of water for a long time. It feeds on nearly anything, including small fishes, shrimps, mollusks, worms, and so on.

Out of water it is aggressive and may attempt to bite its captor. It is not considered an edible variety of fish.

ORDER *Gadiformes*

CODFISHES — FAMILY *Gadidae*

The Gadidae are a large family of soft-rayed fishes of great commercial importance throughout the world.

Atlantic cod[7]
Cod, codfish, rock cod
Gadus morhua Linnaeus
Gadus callarias Linnaeus

SIZE: Varies greatly with location and depth. Atlantic cod weighing over 200 pounds are on record. A specimen over 4 feet long is a large offshore fish; they run somewhat smaller inshore.

COLOR: Gray, gray-green, green-brown, or brown to red-brown above; lighter on sides; whitish beneath; upper half of body spotted, lateral line white. Color varies with diet and habitat; "rock cod" refers to a small, reddish cod.

RANGE: From the northernmost part of our range south to New Jersey. The largest populations are found from Labrador to Nantucket. Ranges somewhat farther southward in the winter than in the summer.

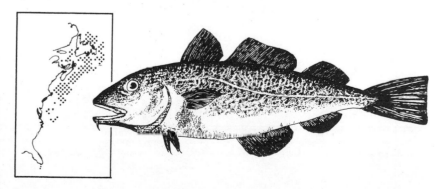

The Atlantic cod may well be the most important food fish in the world. Few major nations have not launched fishing fleets to seek the cod in the North Atlantic. As far back as 1945, in excess of 70 million pounds of codfish were harvested by the United States alone.

Atlantic cod are prolific. A large female may spawn as many as 9,000,000 eggs, the average one producing from 3 to 4 million. The young grow rapidly, often reaching a length of 1 foot in a year.

The Atlantic cod's diet is varied. It consists primarily of mollusks (such as snails, clams, and squid) but also includes starfish, crabs, and lobsters, as well as other invertebrates and fishes. Young Atlantic cod, which are called "scrod," occasionally fall victim to larger cod.

The Atlantic cod is easily distinguishable by its three rounded dorsal fins, slightly rounded caudal fin, and distinct chin barbels.

The larger Atlantic cod often become the prey of spiny dogfish and other sharks, while the young are gobbled up by a variety of carnivorous fishes, pollock in particular.

Atlantic tomcod
Tomcod, frostfish
Microgadus tomcod Walbaum

SIZE: Ordinarily 10 to 12 inches, occasionally reaching a length of 15 inches.

COLOR: Olive or brown-green with mottling above; brown-green to yellow-green with dark mottling and blotches on the sides; off-white to yellow-white beneath; fins mottled.

RANGE: Nova Scotia to Virginia.

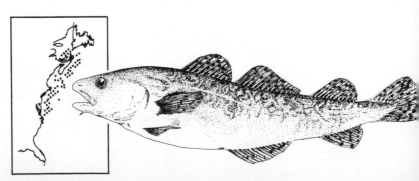

The Atlantic tomcod at first glance looks like a pocket-sized version of the codfish, but on closer examination the tomcod is seen to have more rounded first dorsal and caudal fins than the cod.

M. tomcod is an inshore fish found around breakwaters and piers. It is a delicious food fish and was, when its numbers were greater, particularly important to commercial fisheries. Overfishing and pollution have reduced the tomcod's numbers in the last dozen years.

Haddock
Melanogrammus aeglefinus Linnaeus

SIZE: Usually from 12 to 24 inches long; specimens to 44 inches have been recorded.

COLOR: Back and upper sides dark purple-gray; lighter and silvery below the lateral line; belly white.

RANGE: Newfoundland to Cape Cod, ranging as far south as New Jersey in winter, occasionally as far south as North Carolina in deep water.

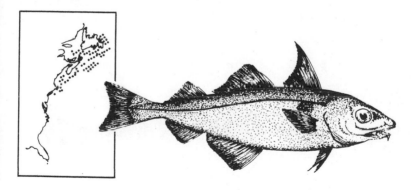

The haddock has a dark lateral line as opposed to the cod and pollock, which have light lateral lines. Its first dorsal fin is pointed and it has a distinct blotch (historically referred to as the "devil's mark") directly behind the gills and above the pectorals.

The haddock mixes with codfish but has a tendency to wander farther south. It is not as likely to be found in shoal waters as are either cod or pollock.

As the more popular fish such as flounder and salmon have drastically declined in numbers, the economic value of haddock has increased. Even so, overfishing of the species, as well as the disturbance of its spawning grounds, threaten the future of the haddock.

Pollock
Pollack, American pollock, Boston bluefish
Pollachius virens Linnaeus

SIZE: The record length is 3½ feet; the average length somewhat less.

COLOR: Deep blue-green, gray-green, or olive-green above; sides paler below the lateral line, becoming silver-gray beneath; ventral fins white to light pink; other fins olive.

RANGE: Usually from Nova Scotia to Long Island; may wander somewhat north and south of these limits.

The pollock has always had a foothold in the commercial fisheries, particularly in Maine. In many markets and restaurants it is sold as "Boston bluefish," though it is not a true bluefish (*P. saltatrix,* see p. 148).

Aside from its consistently green-hued coloration, the pollock can be distinguished by its light lateral line, a more deeply forked caudal fin than is found in either the cod or the haddock, a small second anal fin, very small ventral fin, and a pointed head.

The pollock spawns in the late autumn. The average ripe female carries over 200,000 eggs, while a very large specimen may contain in excess of 4,000,000.

Pollock live in water of any depth and can be caught from breakwaters as well as well out at sea.

Silver hake[8]
Whiting, New England hake
Merluccius bilinearis Mitchill

SIZE: Averages less than 2 feet in length, rarely exceeds 2½ feet.

COLOR: Deep gray above, with bluish reflections; sides silver with a yellowish hue; belly silver to gold.

RANGE: South Carolina north to southern Newfoundland.

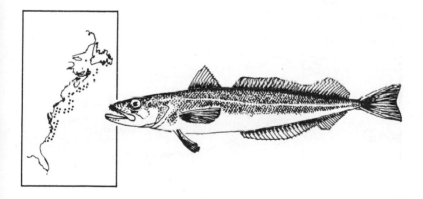

The hake is distinguished from the other codfishes by having two instead of three dorsal fins. The hake's anal fin is situated underneath the second dorsal, and these two fins are about

the same length and shape. The silver hake differs from other
hakes by lacking chin barbels.

These are generally deep-water fish, though the young may
be found at fairly shallow depths.

Silver hake are excellent food fish but are so soft-fleshed that
they have not, until the advent of modern fishing gear and on-
board freezing equipment, been commercially sought after to
any large degree. They are occasionally caught by sports fishermen by bottom-fishing.

Silver hake prey on a variety of small fishes including herring, mackerel, and silversides.

Spotted hake
Spotted ling
Urophycis regius Walbaum
Phycis regius Walbaum

SIZE: Reaches 18 inches in length.

COLOR: Dark brown above, light brown beneath.

RANGE: Normally from Florida to Cape Cod, rounds the Cape on
rare occasions.

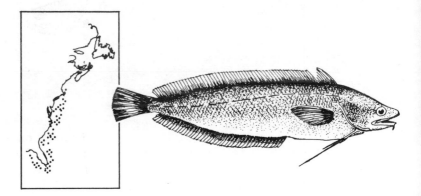

The spotted hake has chin barbels but lacks the streamer on
the first dorsal fin found in several other hakes. It has elongated
spots along the lateral line.

Its diet consists almost exclusively of fishes, but it will subsist on other marine foods in the absence of adequate fish populations. The spotted hake is a winter breeder.

White hake
Mud hake, ling, Boston ling
Urophycis tenuis Mitchill
Phycis tenuis Mitchill

SIZE: Sometimes reaches 4 feet in length, but 2 feet is more common.

COLOR: Purple-brown to gray-brown above; belly cream to yellow, with small black spots. Color varies with environment.

RANGE: North Carolina north to Newfoundland.

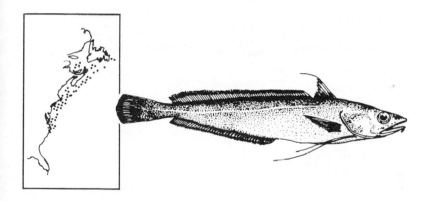

The mud hake* may be identified by the short filament on its first dorsal fin; by stringlike ventral fins that extend to the vent; and by its size, which is somewhat larger than that of other hakes in our area. It is a nocturnal-feeding fish, accepting a variety of foods, including fish, shrimp, and squid. The mud hake spawns in the summer.

* Though the American Fisheries Society has designated the name in boldface type as the "official common name," this name is, in the author's opinion, still more widely used.

Red hake
Squirrel ling, squirrel hake
Urophycis chuss Walbaum
Phycis chuss Walbaum

SIZE: Reaches 30 inches in length.

COLOR: A reddish fish with a greenish back with spots and blotches; white belly; fins mottled.

RANGE: Ordinarily from North Carolina to the St. Lawrence River, strays to Newfoundland.

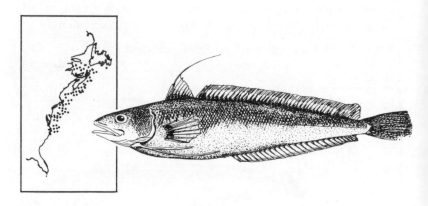

The squirrel hake* sports a distinct filament on the first dorsal fin. It has long, filamentous ventrals, and the mouth does not extend as far back as the rear margin of the eye.

It is excellent on the table and popular with sports fishermen and professionals alike. New, highly successful fishing methods have significantly reduced its numbers.

Squirrel hake may be found from the shoreline to waters over 170 fathoms in depth. The squirrel hake spawns in the summer.

* Though the American Fisheries Society has designated the name in boldface type as the "official common name," this name is, in the author's opinion, still more widely used.

Longfin hake
Phycis chesteri Goode and Bean
Urophycis chesteri Goode and Bean

SIZE: Averages 12 inches long.

COLOR: Green-brown above and on sides, white beneath.

RANGE: Newfoundland to North Carolina.

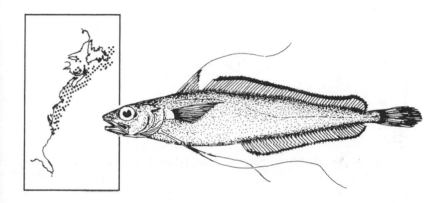

The longfin hake is named for the long ray on the first dorsal fin and the long, filamentous ventral fins, which reach as far back as the caudal peduncle. The caudal fin is long and well rounded.

This is a deep-water hake and quite abundant on the offshore fishing grounds from time to time. It has been found in water of over 500 fathoms.

The longfin have been captured with eggs during the summer and autumn.

Fourbeard rockling
Enchelyopus cimbrius Linnaeus

SIZE: Average length 8 to 10 inches, specimens of over 16 inches have been recorded.

COLOR: Olive-brown to yellow-brown above, lighter on the sides; belly white with small spots.

RANGE: Nova Scotia to Florida.

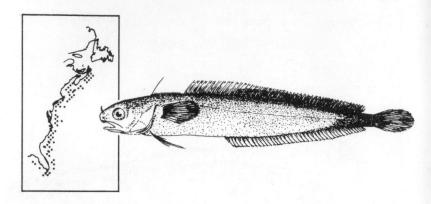

This is the only fish in the Family Gadidae that has a single ray as the first dorsal fin, followed by a row of unconnected rays that can be folded into a groove along the back. The second dorsal, caudal, and anal fins are typical of other hakes. Its name comes from the barbels about the mouth, both above and below.

It is a fine table fish but its small size and scarcity keep it from supporting a commercial market.

Rocklings are found in very shallow waters as well as at depths of several hundred fathoms. In their diet they are partial to shrimps, other small crustaceans, and, occasionally, small fishes.

Cusk
Torsk
Brosme brosme Müller

SIZE: Sometimes exceeds 3 feet in length, with lengths of $2\frac{1}{2}$ feet or less more common.

COLOR: Brown or gray-brown to yellow-brown; lighter sides;

dirty white beneath. Color may vary somewhat depending upon habitat.

RANGE: Usually from Newfoundland to Cape Cod, but is occasionally found in Long Island waters, and on rare occasions it reaches New Jersey.

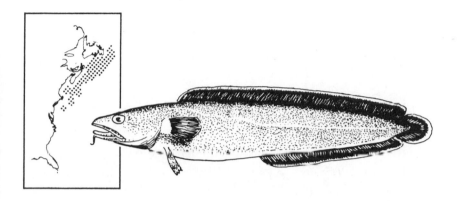

A single long dorsal fin stretching from just behind the origin of the pectoral fins to the base of the caudal fin clearly distinguishes the cusk from other fish in its family. It is flattened sideways, its mouth extends beyond the eyes, and the fins are thick and fleshy.

A significant market exists for cusk, particularly from Long Island northward, as cusk prefer the cooler waters of the continental slope of New England. The sports fisherman rarely seeks them because of their preference for deep water, as much as 500 fathoms or more. Their normal diet includes crabs, clams, and squid. Cusk spawn during the spring and early summer in water over 100 fathoms deep.

CUSK-EELS — FAMILY *Ophidiidae*

Fawn cusk-eel
Cusk-eel
Lepophidium cervinum Goode and Bean

SIZE: Averages 10 to 12 inches in length.

COLOR: Brown-yellow above, lighter below; rows of light spots extend longitudinally on the upper sides; fins have a dark margin; young specimens lack the spots.

RANGE: From off Cape Cod to Florida.

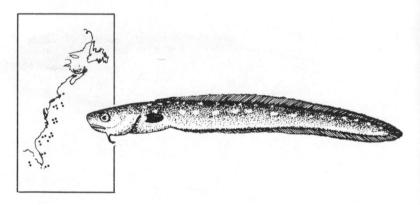

The cusk-eel's continuous dorsal, caudal, and anal fins resemble those of an eel, but the modified ventral fins, which look like chin barbels, as well as a very short but distinct spine on the top of the head ahead of the eyes, distinguish it.

Cusk-eels show a preference for the waters of the outer continental shelf.

OCEAN POUTS OR EELPOUTS — FAMILY *Zoarcidae*

Ocean pout
Eelpout, mutton fish
Macrozoarces americanus Bloch and Schneider

SIZE: Averages 1½ to 2 feet in length, recorded to over 3 feet.

COLOR: Variable in color, commonly a dull reddish-brown with green-brown mottlings, or a yellow-brown with various dark markings; belly nearly white.

RANGE: Newfoundland to New Jersey.

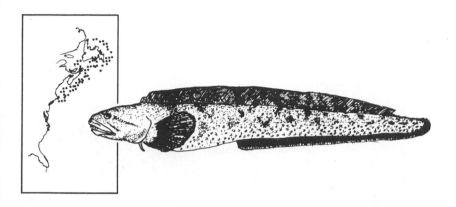

The dorsal, caudal, and anal fins are continuous, though the last couple of dozen dorsal fin rays are so short as to be nearly invisible. The pectoral fins are large and rounded; the ventrals are very small and situated ahead of the pectorals. The mouth is well toothed.

The ocean pout has, from time to time, been of interest in the commercial fisheries. It is marketed under various names.

GRENADIERS — FAMILY *Macrouridae*

There are three grenadiers in our range: the common grenadier (*M. bairdi*), the rough-headed grenadier (*M. berglax*), and the longnose grenadier (*C. carminatus*). They are all very similar in general appearance and are represented here by *M. bairdi*.

Marlin-spike
Rat-tail, common grenadier
Macrourus bairdi Goode and Bean
Nezumia bairdi Goode and Bean

SIZE: Averages 1 foot in length.

COLOR: Generally gray above and below.

RANGE: Mainly from Newfoundland south to Cape Cod; ranges farther south in deep water; strays have been recorded inshore.

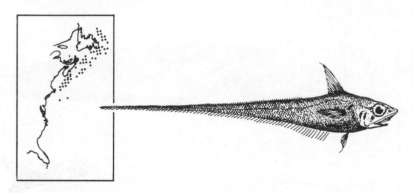

This is a northern deep-water fish. Its lack of a caudal fin; its long- and short-rayed second dorsal and anal fins; and its large head clearly separate it from other fishes in our area.

Common marlin-spikes spawn during the summer months and feed chiefly on small marine invertebrates. They are an abundant species on the slopes off New England.

ORDER *Atheriniformes* (Beloniformes, Synentognathi, Cyprinodontiformes, Microcyprini)

HALFBEAKS AND FLYINGFISHES — FAMILY *Exocoetidae*

In spite of the obvious differences in appearance, the halfbeaks and flyingfishes are currently assigned to a single family.

HALFBEAKS

These fishes are primarily tropical, but one species ranges well within our area.

Halfbeak
Skipjack
Hyporhamphus unifasciatus Ranzani

SIZE: Averages close to a foot in length.

COLOR: Translucent green above, with a bright silver band running from the pectoral fin to the middle of the caudal fin; light cream and silver mixed on the lower sides and belly.

RANGE: A southern fish, uncommon north of Cape Hatteras.

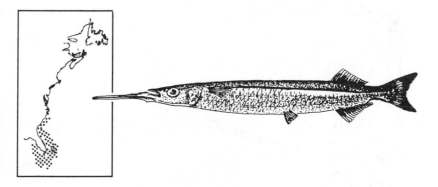

The halfbeaks differ from the needlefishes (Belonidae) by having the upper jaw considerably shorter than the lower. The pectoral fin is high on the body and the dorsal fin is directly over the anal and situated well back on the body.

They have been reported to be a good table fish.

FLYINGFISHES

Flyingfishes have one dorsal and one anal fin placed well rearward, and a deeply forked caudal fin with the lower lobe longer than the upper. They have extremely large pectoral fins, which enable them to glide through the air.

There are several species that may be found in our range. The two described here are the most common and are typical of the family.

Atlantic flyingfish
Common flyingfish
Cypselurus heterurus Rafinesque

SIZE: Attains an overall length of about 15 inches.

COLOR: Dark gray-blue above; silver sides and belly; the rear margin of the pectoral fins has a thin white border.

RANGE: Mainly from Florida to Long Island, occasionally to Cape Cod; reported to Newfoundland, although rarely.

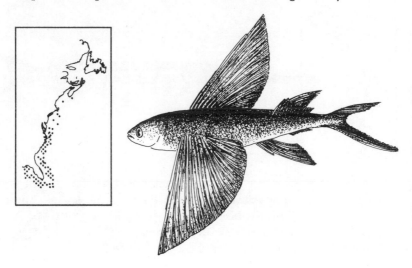

Flyingfishes don't actually fly but are capable of gliding long distances: the larger the fish the longer the distances. The fish swims near the surface for some distance to attain enough speed so that when it spreads its pectorals it will leave the water. As it becomes airborne, the long lower lobe of the caudal fin skims along the surface momentarily to attain even more speed. The Pacific flyingfishes, because of their larger, stronger bodies, have been observed to glide distances of 1000 feet and more; the smaller Atlantic flyingfishes somewhat less.

These fishes are excellent eating though rarely sought after. Sports fishermen occasionally take them on small flies. They are also netted at night after being attracted by lights.

Flyingfishes spawn rafts of eggs, which attach to floating seaweed or other objects. The young, when hatched, cluster together, looking like a clump of seaweed.

Smallwing flyingfish
Short-winged flyingfish
Oxyporhamphus micropterus Valenciennes
Parexocoetus mesogaster Bloch

SIZE: Usually to 7 inches.

COLOR: Nearly identical in coloration to the Atlantic flyingfish.

RANGE: Chiefly from Florida to North Carolina, occasionally north to Long Island.

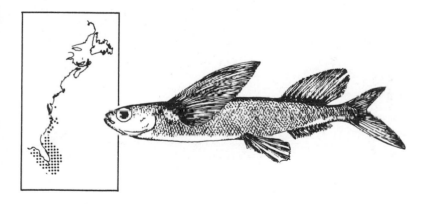

The smallwinged flyingfish, as its name implies, has the smallest pectoral or "wing" fins of the flyingfishes in our range.

The habits of this flyingfish are very similar to those of *C. het-erurus*. Though it is somewhat smaller, it is a fairly good food fish.

NEEDLEFISHES (BILLFISHES) — FAMILY *Belonidae*

Needlefishes have elongated jaws of nearly equal length. They are primarily a tropical family but are represented by two common species in our area.

Atlantic needlefish
Silver gar, saltwater gar, billfish
Strongylura marina Walbaum
Tylosurus marina Walbaum

SIZE: A needlefish 4 feet long is about maximum; usually they run somewhat smaller, especially in the northern regions.

COLOR: Deep green to gray-green above; silver, with a blue-silver longitudinal stripe, on the side; white beneath; bills usually a darker green than the body.

RANGE: Northern Maine to Florida.

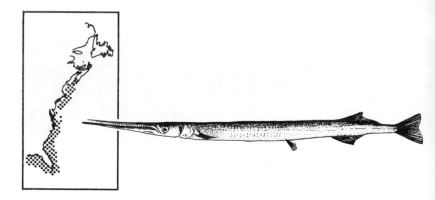

Long, pointed, well-toothed jaws and long, slim bodies with the dorsal and anal fins set well back, are the salient characteristics of the Atlantic needlefish.

The Atlantic needlefish is edible but is rarely sought for the table because of the green tint of its bones and flesh.

Strangely enough these fishes, the larger ones in particular, present a real danger to man. When startled, especially at night, they leap at random from the water, at high speeds. Anyone in the way of these living javelins risks serious injury.

The Atlantic needlefish will often run up freshwater rivers. When caught on sportfishing gear they put up a strong fight.

Flat needlefish
Garfish
Ablennes hians Cuvier and Valenciennes

SIZE: Occasionally exceeds 3 feet in length.

COLOR: Blue-green or green above; silver sides and abdomen; fins and sides sometimes blotched, spotted, or faintly barred.

RANGE: Mainly from Long Island south; known off the south shore of Cape Cod.

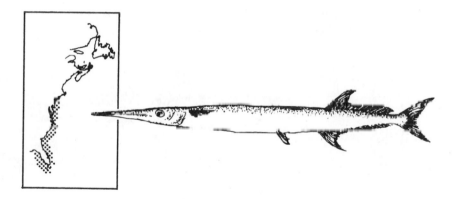

The garfish* is distinguished from other needlefishes in our area by being distinctly laterally compressed, much like a flat-

---

* Though the American Fisheries Society has designated the name in boldface type as the "official common name," this name is, in the author's opinion, still more widely used.

tened hot dog. The jaws of this long, slim fish are of equal length. Its dorsal fin, which originates about two-thirds of the way along the back and slightly behind the anal fin, is long and nearly reaches the caudal fin.

SAURIES (NEEDLEFISHES) — FAMILY *Scomberesocidae*

Atlantic saury
Billfish, needlefish, skipper saury
Scomberesox saurus Walbaum

SIZE: Normally to 18 inches long; a specimen of 30 inches has been recorded.

COLOR: Olive-green above, silver beneath; a silver band runs from the gill covers to the caudal fin at eye level; the dorsal fin is a transparent green. Young saurys are bluish.

RANGE: Throughout our range.

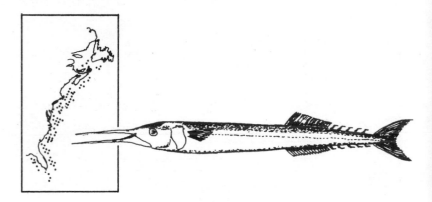

The Atlantic saury looks similar to the needlefishes at first glance, but the presence of dorsal and anal finlets clearly differentiates it from them.

The unpredictable behavior of these fish makes them difficult to seek commercially, though they are excellent for the table. Small ones are popular as bait. Floating eggs are spawned in the warmer seas. Young saurys have short bills.

KILLIFISHES (MUMMICHOGS) — FAMILY *Cyprinodontidae*

Killifishes may be recognized by their small size; single, soft-rayed dorsal fin; small mouth; and thick caudal fin.

Mummichog
Common killifish, saltwater minnow, chub, killie, mummie
Fundulus heteroclitus Linnaeus

SIZE: Averages 3½ inches long as an adult, recorded to 6 inches.

COLOR: Males vary from dark green or green-blue to blue with weak yellow and white spots above, silver lines and irregular markings on the sides, orange-yellow to white below. Colors are markedly more brilliant during the breeding season. Females are uniformly olive-green to brown-green, with faint, dark vertical bars on the sides.

RANGE: Gulf of St. Lawrence and south.

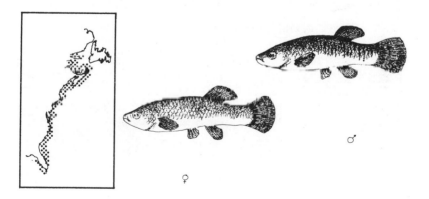

The mummichog, or common killifish, is a coastal fish common in estuaries, harbors, and tidal creeks. It is found as well in bays and salt marshes, rarely venturing more than 100 yards from shore. *F. heteroclitus* can withstand a wide range of temperatures and salinities. It is tolerant, too, of oxygen-depleted water.

Mummichogs are omnivorous feeders subsisting on vegetation, small marine invertebrates, and even carrion. Their presence in the marshes is welcome as they readily feed on mosquito larvae.

Spawning occurs during the summer months, in the shallows.

Striped killifish
Striped mummichog, banded killifish, killie, mummie
Fundulus majalis Walbaum

SIZE: Frequently reaches 6 inches in length, but rarely exceeds 7 inches.

COLOR: The male is dark olive-green above; sides silver with faint vertical bars, sometimes with a gold tinge; belly light yellow-green. There is a dark dot on the posterior portion of the dorsal fin. The colors in the male become more brilliant during the mating season. The female is olive-green above, white or off-white below, and has 2 or 3 dark, irregular longitudinal bars.

RANGE: Cape Cod and southward.

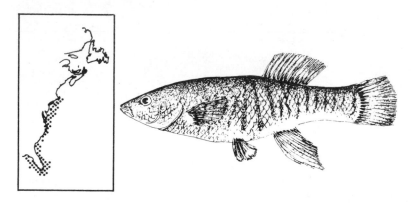

The striped killifish is the largest killifish in our area. It is an omnivorous feeder, disdaining little in the way of food. A shore dweller, it spawns near or in the shallows. It is more likely to be found on the open beaches than in estuaries and marshes.

The striped mummichog has a longer, more pointed snout than the common mummichog and is overall a slimmer fish.

Spawning takes place during spring, summer, and early autumn, near the shore.

Sheepshead minnow
Broad killifish, variegated minnow, killie, mummie
Cyprinodon variegatus Lacépède

SIZE: To 3 inches in length.

COLOR: Brown-green above; yellow to cream beneath; pale orange pectoral fins. Young fish and females have dark vertical bars; males are generally darker, and during the breeding season their backs become steel blue and their bellies red-orange.

RANGE: Cape Cod and southward.

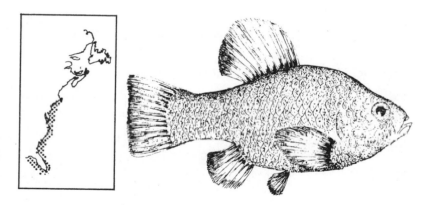

No other killifish is so deep-bodied or has large wedge-shaped teeth like those of the sheepshead. It is the only member of its family in our range with the dorsal fin wholly forward of the anal fin.

The sheepshead prefers bays, estuaries, tidal creeks, and so on. It commonly enters brackish water; like other killies it tolerates a wide range of environmental conditions. It is popular with the sports fisherman as a bait fish.

It spawns from April to September in shallow water.

SILVERSIDES — FAMILY *Atherinidae*

These small, silvery fishes differ from smelts by having much smaller mouths, one spiny and one soft-rayed dorsal fin, and no adipose fin. They are an important forage fish for the predatory species.

Throughout their ranges the silversides have various importance. Generally their soft flesh makes them unsuitable for bait, but their mere presence attracts larger game fish such as stripers and bluefish. The silversides are also a tasty pan fish and can be preserved by pickling and other means.

Atlantic silverside
Common silverside, whitebait, sand smelt, shiner, green smelt
Menidia menidia[9] Linnaeus

SIZE: Occasionally reaches 6 inches in length.

COLOR: Blue-green to olive-green above; upper half of sides speckled with brown spots; dark-bordered silver streak running from the pectoral fin to the middle of the base of the caudal fin; white beneath.

RANGE: Nova Scotia to Florida.

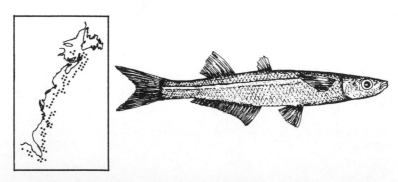

The Atlantic silverside is a slender fish and has large, loose scales. It has a small first dorsal fin and a long anal fin. The pectoral fins are set high on the body. It lacks an adipose fin.

Tidewater silverside
Waxen silverside, whitebait
Menidia beryllina Cope

SIZE: Rarely exceeds 3 inches in length.

COLOR: Gray-green with brown spots above; silver sides and belly; distinct, dark-edged silver band running from pectoral fin to caudal fin.

RANGE: Cape Cod to South Carolina.

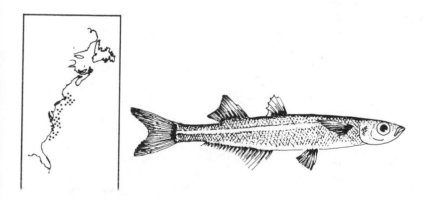

This silverside closely resembles *M. menidia* but can be distinguished from it by the shorter anal fin, which has only 15 or 16 rays as opposed to over 20 rays in the Atlantic silverside. It prefers warmer water than the Atlantic silverside.

ORDER *Zeiformes* (Zeomorphi)

JOHN DORIES — FAMILY *Zeidae*

American john dory
Zenopsis ocellata Storer

SIZE: Averages about 18 inches, but records list specimens exceeding this length.

COLOR: Top, sides, and belly silvery; young fish have some faint, irregular dark spots.

RANGE: Nova Scotia to the Chesapeake Bay.

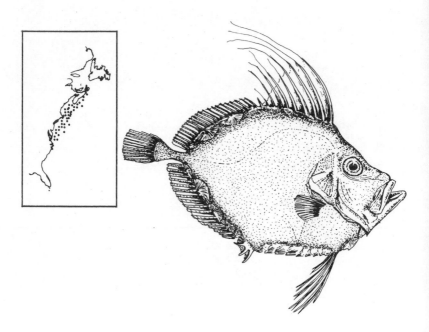

The john dory is a deep-water fish occasionally straying into range of fishing boats.

The upturned mouth; long, free rays of the first dorsal and

ventral fins; thin caudal peduncle; and bony plates on the dorsal and ventral margins are unmistakable field marks of the john dory. Its body is strongly flattened sideways.

John dories feed on fish and various mollusks such as squid.

ORDER *Lampridiformes* (Zeomorphi)

OPAHS — FAMILY *Lamprididae*

Opah
Moonfish
Lampris regius Bonnaterre
Lampris luna Gmelin

SIZE: Reaches 6 feet in length, but commonly 3 to 4 feet.

COLOR: Silvery body with blue and purple hues, darker and more bluish above; red and pink beneath, covered with white and silver spots; fins are shades of red. Colors rapidly fade upon death.

RANGE: Mainly from Newfoundland to Cape Cod, but shows up rather unpredictably in various locations.

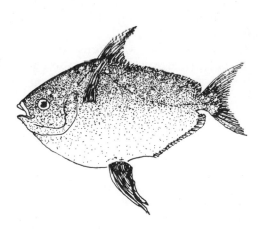

This offshore fish is mentioned here because it more than occasionally wanders into coastal waters and is from time to time caught by fishermen fairly near the shore.

The opah is a laterally compressed fish, almost disklike in appearance. Its lateral line arches over the pectoral fin; its small mouth is toothless; the scales are minute; and it has more rays (14 or more) than any of the mackerels or pompanos.

Opahs feed on a variety of foods, including small fishes, squids, and even seaweeds.

In Europe the opah is a popular food fish. It is not populous enough to support any kind of commercial fishery in the United States or Canada.

ORDER *Gasterosteiformes* (Thoracostei, Hemibranchii, Lophobranchii, Solenichthyes)

STICKLEBACKS — FAMILY *Gasterosteidae*

Sticklebacks are distinguished from all other marine fishes in our area by possessing, ahead of the dorsal fin, two or more free dorsal spines that can be erected at will. They are small fish (a few inches long) and their ventral fins are spikelike.

The male usually builds a cylindrical nest of aquatic vegetation and debris. The female enters the nest depositing eggs, which the male fertilizes. The male defends the nest vigorously until hatching, which may take place from 6 to 12 days after incubation.

Sticklebacks are voracious eaters and with their fanglike teeth are a match for a variety of other species. We can be especially thankful for their habit of favoring mosquito larvae as food.

Ninespine stickleback
Tenspine stickleback
Pungitius pungitius Linnaeus

SIZE: Generally about 2 inches in length, occasionally reaching 3 inches.

COLOR: Olive-brown above, with faint mottling; silvery with dark markings beneath. During the breeding season the markings are more pronounced, and the colors brighter.

RANGE: Frequents the northern part of our range, in both fresh and salt water. Rarely found farther south than Delaware.

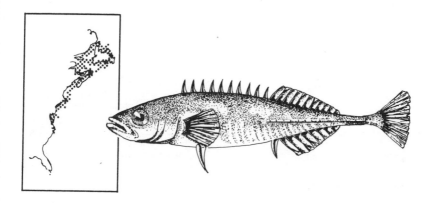

From seven to eleven, but usually nine free spines ahead of the dorsal fin; a deep, segmented keel on the caudal peduncle; and a smooth skin identify this stickleback. It has a large, heavy-lipped, upward-opening mouth.

The ninespine is a particularly pugnacious fish. It will readily attack the spawn and young of other sticklebacks. It is a wide-ranging stickleback, occurring on the coasts of Europe and Alaska as well as in our area.

Threespined stickleback
Thornfish, twospine[10] stickleback
Gasterosteus aculeatus Linnaeus

SIZE: Rarely exceeds 4 inches in length; from $2\frac{1}{2}$ to 3 inches is common.

COLOR: Variable in color; shows more red than other sticklebacks, especially during the breeding season. The platelike scales on the sides impart a silvery luster.

RANGE: Well represented from Nova Scotia to the Chesapeake Bay, occasionally straying somewhat north and south of these limits.

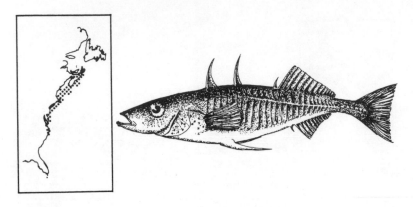

The threespine stickleback remains close to shore readily ascending freshwater streams, where it is equally at home. It is a voracious feeder, eating nearly anything obtainable.

This stickleback is distinguished by three free dorsal spines, two large and one small, by distinct plates on its side; and by a small keel on the caudal peduncle.

The reputation sticklebacks have for building elaborate nests is probably best earned by the threespine stickleback. The male makes a barrel-shaped nest in freshwater vegetation and proceeds to escort a number of females to it. They, in turn, push their way through the nest, laying a number of eggs inside it. The male guards the nest and the young until they can venture out on their own.

Fourspine stickleback
Bloody stickleback
Apeltes quadracus Mitchill

SIZE: Usually from 1½ to 2 inches; rarely to 2½ inches.

COLOR: Brown-green with dark mottling above; silver white on the belly; soft part of ventral fin red. Females lighter colored.

RANGE: Common from Nova Scotia to Cape Cod; less common as far south as Virginia.

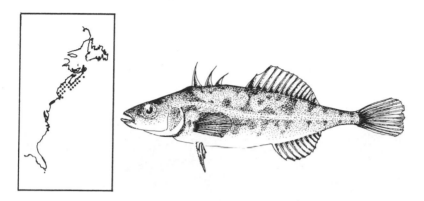

The fourspine stickleback, *A. quadracus,* is easily distinguishable from other sticklebacks by being more laterally compressed, lacking a keel on the caudal peduncle, and having a sawtoothed edge on the ventral fins. It may have from 2 to 4 free dorsal spines.

It is a coastal fish preferring estuarine and salt marsh habitats. It may ascend streams to freshwater pools, but not as readily as other sticklebacks.

The male builds a small, modest nest. The eggs hatch in about a week of incubation.

SEAHORSES — FAMILY *Syngnathidae*

There are five seahorses indigenous to the Atlantic coast: the northern seahorse *(H. hudsonius)*, the lined or spotted seahorse *(H. erectus)*, the offshore seahorse *(H. obtusus)*, the longsnout seahorse *(H. reidi)*, and the dwarf seahorse *(H. zosterae)*. They are represented here by the northern seahorse.

Lined seahorse
Northern seahorse, seahorse
Hippocampus erectus Perry
Hippocampus hudsonius DeKay

SIZE: Averages 3 to 6 inches from head to tail.

COLOR: Yellow-brown, gray-brown to gray, light and dark spots and mottling. Color and marking varies greatly with habitat.

RANGE: Generally South Carolina to Cape Cod, occasionally to the Gulf of Maine. May range as far south as northern Florida.

This curious fish is unusual not only in appearance, but in habits as well. In shape it strongly resembles a legless horse or a knight in a chess set; it is covered with bony plates; it lacks ventral and caudal fins.

The male has a small pouch on its abdomen where the female lays as many as 150 eggs, though not all at once. They are cared for by the male until they are hatched and have absorbed the yolk sacs. The male then ejects them to fend for themselves.

Seahorses of various species are frequently kept in aquariums but require more care than is usually given to tropical saltwater fish.

They feed upon small marine life, which they suck in through their pipelike mouths.

This family also includes another unusual group of fishes, the pipefishes. They are characterized by a long tubular snout and "armor"-plated body. It is a group of about 12 species, represented in this book by the northern, or common, pipefish.

Northern pipefish
Common pipefish
Syngnathus fuscus Storer

SIZE: Commonly 4 to 7 inches long, may reach 1 foot.

COLOR: Green-brown to brown above, belly silver, mottling and bars on sides. Color and markings vary with habitat.

RANGE: Nova Scotia to South Carolina.

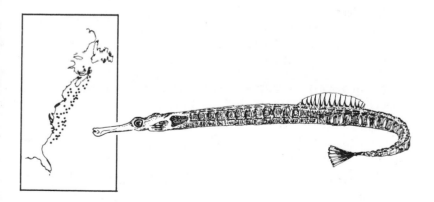

Like the northern, or lined, seahorse, the male pipefish has a pouch on its abdomen in which he incubates and "gives birth" to the young.

Pipefishes are usually found among marine vegetation, particularly eel grass (*Z. marina*), where they search out small marine animals while hiding from their enemies. They prefer coastal waters such as estuaries, mouths of rivers, and brackish waters.

ORDER *Perciformes* (Percomorphi, Acanthopterygii)

TEMPERATE BASSES — FAMILY *Percichthyidae*

Marine basses comprise a large variety of familiar species, including many popular sports fish. Many of these fishes are sought commercially.

They are characterized by spiny rays and a soft portion of the dorsal fin, which appears either as a separate fin or a single fin divided by a notch. They have large scales and smooth cheeks. There are three distinct spines preceding the anal fin.

Marine basses are found in both the Atlantic and Pacific oceans. Within our range they generally occur from the Gulf of St. Lawrence to northern Florida.

Striped bass
Rockfish, striper, lined bass
Morone saxatilis Walbaum
Roccus saxatilis Walbaum

SIZE: On record are a 125-pound striped bass caught off North Carolina (world record), a 112-pounder caught off Cape Cod, and a 73-pounder from Martha's Vineyard Sound. A striper 24 inches in length weighs from 7 to 10 pounds; an individual 3 feet long may exceed 20 pounds.

COLOR: Olive-gray to gray-green above, silver sides, white belly; 7 or 8 longitudinal stripes of varying contrast (stripe becomes less distinct, particularly on the lower sides, with age) running from the gill cover to the caudal fin; dorsal and caudal fins are dusky gray-green. In warmer waters there may be a distinct red tinge on the caudal fin.

RANGE: Striped bass occur on both the Pacific and Atlantic coasts. In our area they range from the Gulf of St. Lawrence to Florida waters.

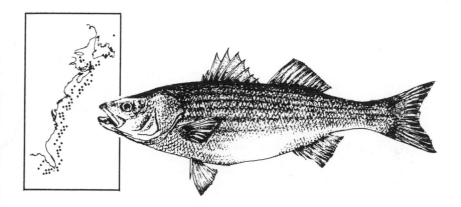

There have been many study programs to research the habits of the striped bass, though there is still some controversy about their spawning grounds. They are an anadromous fish and are known to enter the Chesapeake Bay and its rivers in Maryland, and the Roanoke River in North Carolina to breed. They have been known to spawn in various other river estuaries such as the Hudson and Connecticut.

Stripers "migrate" northward along the east coast in the spring and return southward in the late fall as the water temperatures drop. Local populations may establish their own migratory patterns.

Landlocked populations of the striper have been established, most notably in the Carolinas.

This is a typical-looking bass. It usually has 9 or 10 spines in the first dorsal fin and 12 or 13 soft rays in the well-separated second dorsal. Both fins are about the same height. The anal fin has about 11 soft rays preceded by 3 stiff ones. The caudal fin is distinctly forked.

Fishermen of all ages seek this fish by nearly every known method of fishing, and with an endless array of tackle, from shores, piers, and boats. Stripers are not usually found very far offshore. When caught they put up an impressive struggle; when served at the dinner table they are fit for the epicure.

White perch
Sea perch
Morone americana Gmelin
Roccus americanus Gmelin

SIZE: Averages 8 to 10 inches, reaches a length of 15 inches.

COLOR: Olive to gray-green to gray above; sides lighter becoming white on the belly; variously colored depending upon habitat. Young fish may show faint longitudinal stripes.

RANGE: Nova Scotia to North Carolina.

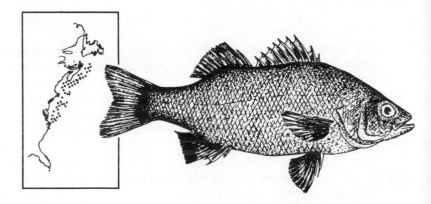

The white perch is a typical temperate bass. Its first and second dorsal fins are separated by a deep notch, and it is deeper bodied and more compressed sideways than the striped bass. A smaller fish than the striper, it lacks longitudinal stripes.

White perch are more populous in restricted bodies of

water—salt, brackish, and fresh—than in the open ocean. They feed on young fishes, small shrimps, crabs, the eggs of other fishes, squids, and a variety of other small marine animals.

Spawning takes place in freshwater streams between April and June.

White perch are easily caught on a variety of tackle. They make excellent table fish.

Wreckfish
Wreckbass
Polyprion americanus Bloch and Schneider

SIZE: Reaches a length of 5 to 6 feet.

COLOR: Gray to gray-brown to black-brown; the caudal fin is edged in white. Juveniles show a mottled pattern.

RANGE: Throughout our range.

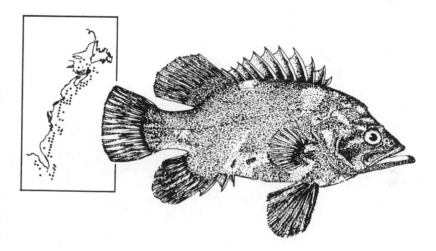

This is not a common fish in our range. It may be distinguished from other members of its family by a rounded caudal fin, a pointed snout, and rough scales. It is considerably flattened sideways (laterally).

It is common to find young wreckfish under floating debris, such as logs or wreckage, hence their common name.

SEA BASSES — FAMILY *Serranidae*[11]

Black sea bass
Blackfish, sea bass
Centropristis striata Linnaeus
Centropristes striatus Linnaeus

SIZE: Grows to a length of 2 feet, commonly much smaller; an 8-pound species is on record.

COLOR: Gray-black, blue-black, or brown on the back and sides; belly lighter; shows some mottling in certain habitats; brilliant yellow to orange beneath the gill covers at the throat. The dorsal fin has light bars.

RANGE: Common from Cape Cod to Florida, sometimes rounds the Cape to the Gulf of Maine.

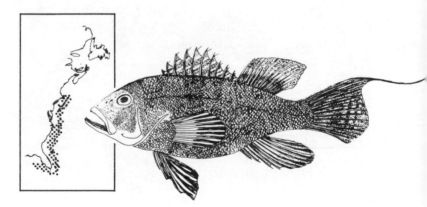

This is a popular bottom fish as it is easily caught with a variety of baits and tackle. It is an excellent table fish as well.

Not only is its dark coloration distinctive, but there are small "flags" on the tops of the spiny rays of the dorsal fin and

a streamer on the top of the caudal. The streamer may be short-
ened or even missing on older fish. The scales are large and have
a dark edge.

Black sea bass are found well inshore during the summer
months. In the winter months they retreat to water over 400 feet
deep.

Spawning takes place in May and June from North Carolina to Cape Cod.

Red grouper
Epinephelus morio Valenciennes

SIZE: Normally up to 3 feet in length; a 4-foot specimen is on
record.

COLOR: Generally mottled with a reddish hue, which is strong at
the base of the jaws and pectoral fins; dark spots about the eyes
and light spots on the head and back. Color and pattern vary
with the habitat.

RANGE: Virginia and southward, but rare north of North Carolina, and not common north of Florida. Commonest in the tropical seas.

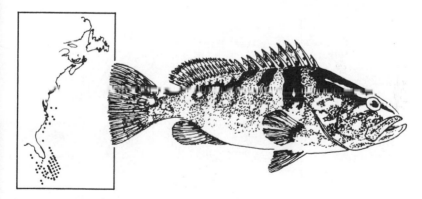

The red grouper is distinguished by a continuous first and
second dorsal fin without a notch between the rays, and a
straight or slightly concave caudal fin.

E. morio is a tropical member of Serranidae, accessible to sports and commercial fishermen in the southernmost reaches of our range. It is a fine table fish.

BIGEYES — FAMILY *Priacanthidae*

This tropical family of fishes is distinguishable from the sea basses by its conspicuously scaled gill covers (opercula) and head. The short bigeye, *P. alta,* is found well within our range.

Short bigeye
Deep bigeye
Pristigenys alta Gill
Pseudopriacanthus altus Gill

SIZE: Larger fish are 8 to 10 inches in length.

COLOR: Appears red all over.

RANGE: Normally tropical, but strays as far north as Cape Cod, and on rare occasions into the Gulf of Maine.

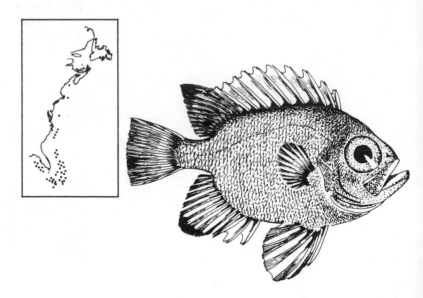

This small, interesting fish is a colorful curiosity when caught. It is disklike in general shape, with comparatively large fins for its size.

Adults are usually found in deep water up to 100 or more fathoms. Eggs are spawned well offshore during the summer months.

TILEFISHES — FAMILY *Branchiostegidae*

Only one species of tilefish occurs in our area. It is characterized by a long second dorsal fin, with a fleshy flap as a first dorsal fin.

Tilefish
Lopholatilus chamaeleonticeps Goode and Bean

SIZE: The maximum weight recorded for a tilefish is 50 pounds, but weights of less than 30 pounds and sizes under 40 inches are to be expected.

COLOR: Green, blue-green, or blue on the back and upper sides; yellow to pink on lower sides; belly white at the apex. Upper sides have small yellow spots; upper side of head reddish marks. Adipose fin yellow-green; dorsal fin spotted; anal fin barred; pectoral fins have a light brown tint.

RANGE: Usually from Nova Scotia to the Chesapeake, but reported as far south as Florida.

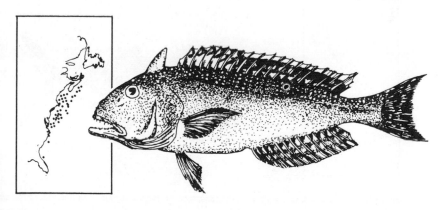

The brilliant colors and the fleshy first dorsal or "adipose" fin are the unmistakable field marks of the tilefish.

They are a good fish for eating and have been of considerable commercial importance. They are not often found in less than 200 feet of water.

The tilefish is a bottom fish which feeds on a variety of marine life, preferring crabs over shrimps, squids, sea anemones, and so on. It spawns in deep water in the summer months.

BLUEFISHES — FAMILY *Pomatomidae*

This family consists of a single species, *P. saltatrix*.

Bluefish
Snapper (young—see frontispiece)
Pomatomus saltatrix Linnaeus

SIZE: Recorded to 45 inches in length, commonly about half of that.

COLOR: Blue to blue-green or blue-gray above, sides lighter, belly silvery to white; snappers are rich blue on the top with a metallic sheen on the sides and a silver-white belly.

RANGE: Commonly from Cape Cod south; may round the Cape and stray as far north as Nova Scotia.

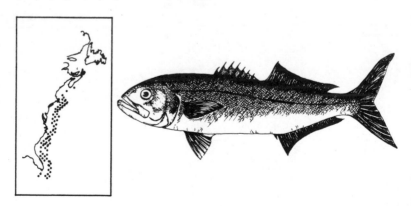

Few fish are as popular as the bluefish both as a food fish and as a sports fish. They are sought after from shore and from boats and support a substantial commercial fishery as well.

Bluefish are voracious feeders, often killing more fish than they can eat. They may travel in schools or wait under tidal rips, snapping up small fish caught in the current. It is not uncommon to find them in company with the bonito (*S. sarda*).

Their small first dorsal fin and deeply forked caudal fin resemble those of some of the jacks (Carangidae), but the bluefish is clearly distinguished by its large, rounded head; long, sharp teeth; lack of bony plates (scutes) ; and smooth caudal peduncle.

Bluefish exhibit a migratory instinct, traveling north along our coast in the spring and returning south in the late fall. Schools of bluefish are made up of fish of nearly the same size, probably because large blues readily attack the young of their own species.

The spawning habits of the bluefish are not well known, but the abundance of young (snappers) in channels, bays, and estuaries suggests that these waters are not far from their usual ranges. The snapper, as well as the adult bluefish, is an excellent table fish.

COBIAS — FAMILY *Rachycentridae*

Cobias range worldwide and are a family of only one species.

Cobia
Sergeantfish, crabeater, ling, cabio, coalfish, black bonito
Rachycentron canadum Linnaeus

SIZE: Reaches a length of 5 feet; a 50-pound cobia is common.

COLOR: Dark brown above, lighter on the sides and belly; a band, which becomes less distinct with age, runs from the eye to the caudal fin.

RANGE: New Jersey and south, rarely strays as far north as the Gulf of Maine.

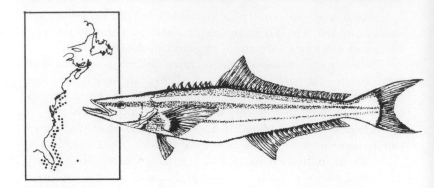

Cobias are a favorite game fish because of their size and their excellent flavor.

The cobia is best described as having a long, flat head with a projecting lower jaw; short, stiff, unconnected spines in the first dorsal fin; and a large pectoral fin. They prey upon most kinds of small fishes as well as shrimps and crabs. They are at home in the open ocean, though young cobia are frequently found close to shore.

REMORAS — FAMILY *Echeneidae*

Remoras are characterized by the highly modified first dorsal fin, which acts as a sucking disk. They are slender fishes, their mouths armed with numerous small, pointed teeth.

Remoras do not necessarily attach to one particular animal only, although the various species usually show a preference for sharks, swordfish, and so on. They may attach to a wide variety of things including even, on occasion, boats.

Sharksucker
Echeneis naucrates Linnaeus

SIZE: Occasionally exceeds 3 feet in length.

COLOR: Gray or brown-gray with a white-bordered dark stripe on the sides extending from the mouth to the caudal fin. The caudal fin is black with white corners.

RANGE: Nova Scotia and southward.

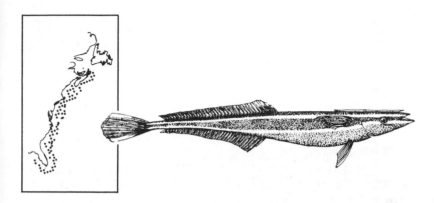

The sharksucker is distinguished by a rounded caudal fin (may not be evident in very old fish), a pointed pectoral fin, 32 to 41 rays in the soft dorsal fin, and 31 to 38 rays in the anal fin.

Big remoras have been used to catch turtles by attaching a line to the base of the tail of the fish and allowing the fish to attach itself to the shell of a sea turtle. The fish is then carefully retrieved with the turtle attached. In its natural life, as the name implies, it is most frequently found on sharks.

Sharksuckers feed on scraps left by their host. They in turn are an excellent food fish.

Spearfish remora
Swordfish remora
Remora brachyptera Lowe

SIZE: Reaches a length of 12 inches.

COLOR: Pale red-brown above, darker beneath.

RANGE: Throughout the southern part of our range, occasionally as far north as Cape Cod.

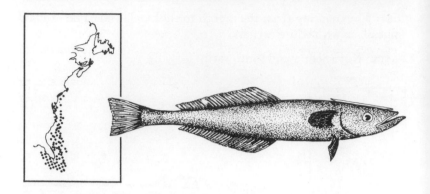

The pectoral fin is rounded; the soft dorsal fin has 29 to 32 rays; the dorsal fins are proportionately shorter and more rounded than the sharksucker's (*E. naucrates*), but not as much as the remora's (*R. remora*). This species of remora is somewhat more heavy bodied than its relatives.

The habits of this remora are not well known, except that it is most commonly found attached to swordfish.

Remora
Common remora
Remora remora Linnaeus

SIZE: Reaches 18 inches in length, but averages less.

COLOR: Overall brown, gray-brown, or nearly black.

RANGE: Long Island and south, commonest in the warmer seas.

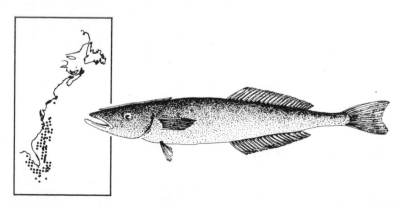

This remora has the shortest and most rounded second dorsal and anal fins of the Echeneidae in our range. It has a moderately rounded tail and 22 to 25 rays in the second dorsal fin.

Very little is known of the life history of this remora, except that it has been found clinging to a variety of fishes and other objects.

POMPANOS AND JACKS — FAMILY *Carangidae*

The Carangidae usually have two dorsal fins, the first smaller than the second, and deeply forked tails.

It is a large family with over 30 species in the western Atlantic alone, most of them in the warm seas. They are mostly strong, fast swimmers and splendid game fish, and many are considered to have excellent-tasting flesh.

For convenience, they can be divided into 7 groups: jacks (includes pilotfish and rudderfishes) ; scads; threadfins; lookdowns; pompanos; amberjacks; and leatherjackets. Threadfins, lookdowns, and leatherjackets are neither abundant nor of great commercial importance in our range.

Round scad
Round robin, mackerel scad
Decapterus punctatus Agassiz

SIZE: Reaches about 12 inches in length.

COLOR: Dull blue to gray-blue above, grayish below; a small black spot is usually present on the posterior edge of the gill cover; lateral line appears as a series of dots.

RANGE: Cape Cod and southward.

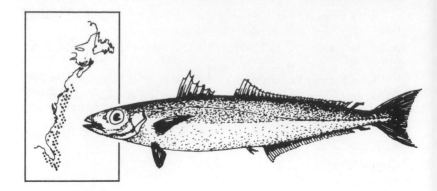

The round scad is mackerellike in appearance but has long second dorsal and anal fins as well as dorsal and anal finlets. It has about 40 pointed scutes in the straight portion of the lateral line, and small, detached dorsal and ventral finlets between the dorsal and caudal fins and the anal and caudal fins, respectively.

Mackerel scad
Round scad
Decapterus macarellus Cuvier and Valenciennes

SIZE: To about 1 foot in length.

COLOR: Dull gray-blue above, lighter beneath.

RANGE: Usually Cape Cod and southward, but occasionally rounds the Cape and has been reported from Nova Scotia.

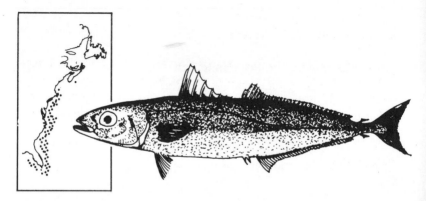

Mackerel scad are occasionally abundant as far north as Cape Cod but prefer warmer waters.

The smooth unbroken lateral line is an obvious field mark distinguishing the mackerel scad from the round scad (*D. punctatus*). It has small, detached finlets between the dorsal and caudal fins and between the anal and caudal fins. There are about 30 scutes in the posterior portion of the lateral line.

Bigeye scad
Goggle-eyed scad, goggle-eye jack
Selar crumenophthalmus Bloch
Trachurops crumenophthalmus Bloch

SIZE: Rarely reaches a length of 2 feet.

COLOR: Blue to blue-gray above, silvery beneath; fins are blotched.

RANGE: Frequents the warmer waters in our range but straggles as far north as Nova Scotia.

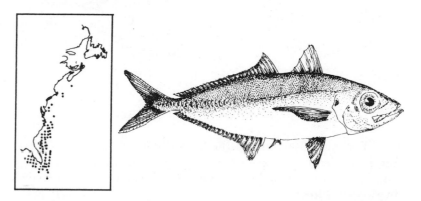

The big-eye scad is named for its oversized eyes. Its lateral line is only slightly arched over the pectoral. It is heavily scaled overall. The scutes are distinct on the posterior half of the lateral line. There are two distinct, free spiny rays ahead of the anal fin.

The big-eye feeds on small fish and a variety of marine invertebrates.

Blue runner
Hard-tailed jack, hardtail, yellow jack, runner
Caranx crysos Mitchill

SIZE: Averages 12 inches in length in the northern and a little over 20 inches in the southern part of its range.

COLOR: Green-yellow with a metallic sheen above, gold to silver sides and belly; usually there is a dark blotch on the gill cover. Young specimens are barred.

RANGE: Frequents waters from Cape Cod south, but straggles as far north as Nova Scotia.

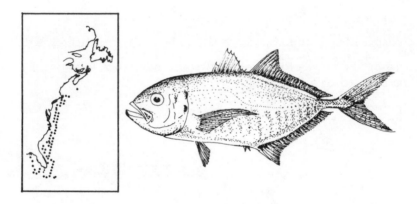

There is a high arch in the lateral line over the pectoral fin; the scutes become larger toward the tail; the second dorsal has one spine followed by 23 to 25 soft rays. The anal fin is preceded by two free spines.

The blue runner, or hardtail, feeds on fishes and shrimps. It is known on both the Pacific and Atlantic coasts of North America.

Jack mackerel
Rough scad, saurel
Trachurus symmetricus Ayres

Trachurus trachurus Linnaeus
Trachurus lathami Nichols

SIZE: Common at 9 inches, and sometimes reaches a length of 1 foot.

COLOR: Blue-green above, lower sides and belly silver.

RANGE: Cape Cod and southward; prefers the warmer waters.

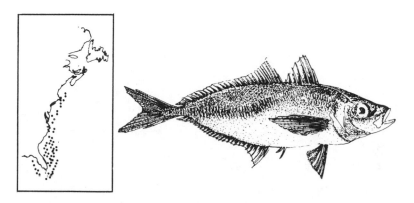

The saurel, more recently called the jack mackerel, is distinguishable from all other Carangidae and Scombridae in our range by its distinct row of about 75 scutes along the entire length of its lateral line. Its first dorsal fin has 8 spiny rays, the second 25 to 30 soft rays.

This is not a common species north of Florida, but it is quite common at times off southern Florida. It feeds largely on small fishes.

Crevalle jack
Jack crevalle, common jack, crevalle, cavalla, toro
Caranx hippos Linnaeus

SIZE: Rarely exceeds 2½ feet in length.

COLOR: Dark blue-green or metallic green above, silver to gold reflections on side and below; anal fin various shades of orange-yellow; the gill cover has a large dark blotch on it. Young specimens may display vertical bars.

RANGE: Uncommon north of Cape Cod, abundant in the southern part of our range.

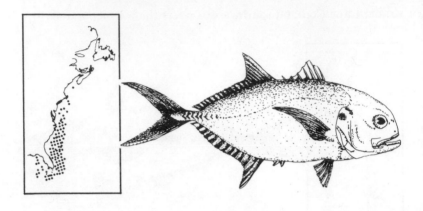

The crevalle may be distinguished by its large, blunt head; prominent first dorsal fin; long, scimitar-shaped pectoral fins; and its eyes that are almost entirely ahead of the posterior margin of the mouth. It has bony shields on either side of the caudal peduncle. Its second dorsal and anal fins are more elongated and pointed than in other Carangidae.

Adult jack crevalles usually travel in schools, though very large specimens sometimes lead a solitary life. Jack crevalles are found in a variety of marine environments, such as bays and estuaries, as well as at sea.

Spawning is believed to take place offshore in the summer months.

This attractive fish is eagerly sought after by sports fishermen because of its fighting ability. It is not reported to be a particularly good food fish, though it is marketed in Florida and Central America.

Yellow jack
Cibi amarillo
Caranx bartholomaei Cuvier and Valenciennes

SIZE: To 15 inches in length; a 39-inch specimen is on record.

COLOR: Overall pearllike appearance with light blue-green upper sides and yellowish fins. Young yellow jacks have vertical bars which develop a mottled pattern that in time diasppears.

RANGE: Cape Cod and south; far more common in the southern part of its range.

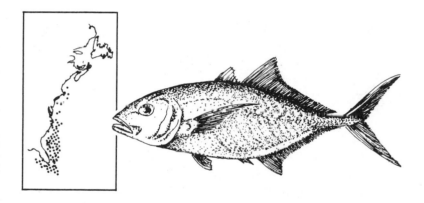

There are about 22 to 28 distinct scutes on the posterior third of the lateral line. The second dorsal fin has one spine followed by 25 to 28 soft rays.

Yellow jacks spawn well offshore, presumably from about February through September.

The yellow jack is considered an excellent sports fish, but only fair as food. It is commercially sought and marketed in the West Indies.

Horse-eye jack
Atlantic horse-eye jack, goggle-eye jack
Caranx latus Agassiz

SIZE: Rarely exceeds 20 inches in length.

COLOR: Deep blue to gray-blue above, white to gold on the sides and beneath; the caudal fin is distinctly yellow.

RANGE: Virginia and southward.

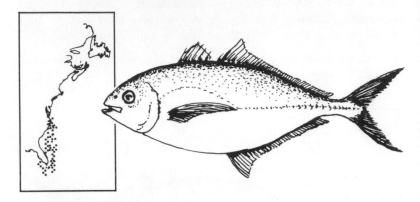

The horse-eye jack has a blunt forehead and scutes that start widening toward the tail, beginning beneath the highest ray of the second dorsal fin. The second dorsal fin is higher than the first and the belly is well scaled.

Horse-eyes feed primarily on fish but sometimes include crabs and shrimps in their diet.

Spawning probably occurs from April through June off the southeastern United States.

This is an excellent game fish but is not placed high on the epicure's list.

African pompano
Threadfish, Atlantic threadfin, Cuban jack[12]
Alectis crinitus Mitchill

SIZE: Can grow to 3 feet, but specimens over 7 inches are unusual in our area.

COLOR: Blue to blue-green above, sides silvery; faint, dark vertical lines present on young specimens.

RANGE: Generally tropical but young specimens stray as far north as Cape Cod.

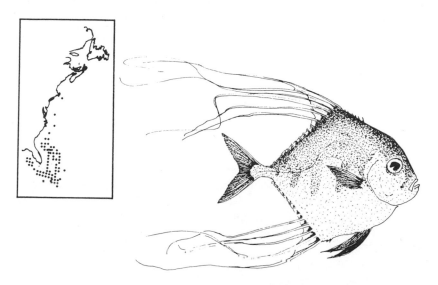

The long threadlike first rays of the soft dorsal and anal fins are distinguishing field marks of the African pompano although older individuals tend to lose them. Those that have entirely lost them are sometimes called "Cuban jacks" (*H. cubensis* Poey). Threadfins are very much flattened laterally.

Threadfins are sought by sports fishermen in tropical waters. They are a popular food fish.

Pilotfish
Shark pilotfish, rudderfish
Naucrates ductor Linnaeus

SIZE: May exceed 2 feet, but is usually somewhat smaller.

COLOR: Bluish-brown to brown above, lighter sides with 5 to 7 wide vertical bands. The caudal fin is white tipped.

RANGE: Widely ranging, but not common north of the Chesapeake Bay.

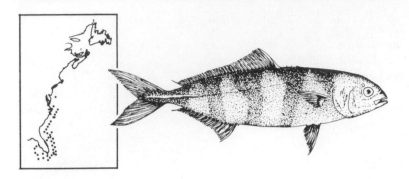

Pilotfish seem to frequent warm-water regions throughout the world. They have the curious habit of keeping close company with sharks and sometimes with boats in the open sea. They have also been reported closely following rays.

The pilotfish is a slimmer fish than most of the Carangidae. It can be distinguished by the small, separate rays of the first dorsal fin.

Pilotfish feed on shark parasites and on scraps left by sharks, as well as a variety of other foods.

Banded rudderfish

Rudderfish, pilotfish, shark pilot, amberjack, slender amberjack
Seriola zonata Mitchill

SIZE: Maximum length about 3 feet.

COLOR: Blue to blue-brown to silver-brown above, with 5 or 6 blue to brown vertical bands, which become indistinct with age. The dorsal fin is greenish, with a white outer margin.

RANGE: Occurs throughout our range, but is not common north of Cape Cod.

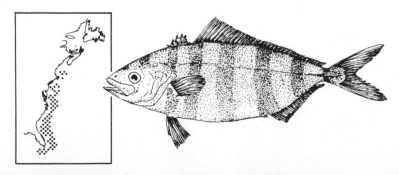

The banded rudderfish is distinguished from the pilotfish, *N. ductor*, by its deeper body and the larger rays (connected by membranes) of the first dorsal fin.

Like the pilotfish, it has earned its name because of its habit of closely following boats and sharks.

Banded rudderfish are often found close to shore, where they are sometimes caught by sports fishermen. Their numbers are too few to support a commercial fishery.

Leatherjacket
Leathercoat
Oligoplites saurus Bloch and Schneider

SIZE: Reaches about a foot in length.

COLOR: Blue to blue-gray above, silver-gray below; the fins are generally yellow.

RANGE: Normally north to Virginia, but straggles as far as Cape Cod.

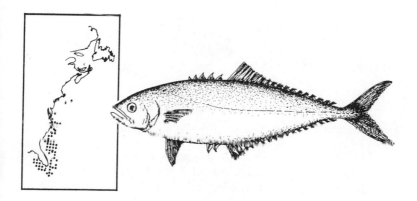

This is a fish of the warm seas that reaches as far as Cape Cod when the water is unusually warm.

Its chief distinguishing features are the second dorsal and anal fins, which separate into coarse finlets on the caudal peduncle.

These fish are found near the coast, close to sandy beaches and in tidal currents. They are not generally sought by fishermen. When caught, they are usually used as bait, as their flesh is dry and bony.

Atlantic moonfish
Moonfish, horsefish, bluntnose, shiner, dollarfish
Vomer setapinnis Mitchill

SIZE: Averages 9 inches in length, recorded to a foot.

COLOR: Blue-green above; silvery sides; pectoral fins yellow to yellow-green.

RANGE: Usually Cape Cod and south, but occasionally strays to the Gulf of Maine. More common in the southern part of its range.

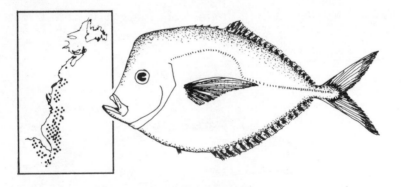

The moonfish has a high forehead and a very deep, thin body. The first dorsal fin consists of 8 short, separate rays.

This is an excellent fish for eating. It is a nocturnal feeder and is common at night around docks and piers in the southern part of our range.

Lookdown
Horsefish, moonfish
Selene vomer Linnaeus

SIZE: Rarely exceeds a foot in length.

COLOR: Iridescent silver; young generally show dark bands.

RANGE: Cape Cod south. Only small ones reach as far north as the Cape.

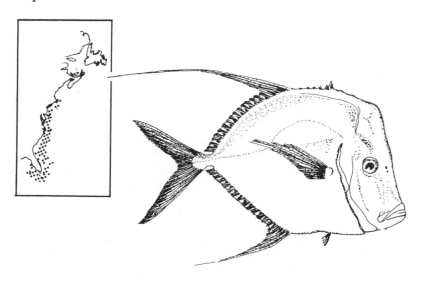

With its high, flat forehead and wafer-thin body, the lookdown is not likely to be confused with any other species in our area. The long first rays of the first dorsal and anal fins distinguish it from the moonfish.

Though not populous enough to be of interest to commercial fishermen, it is eagerly sought by many for its fine-tasting flesh.

Florida pompano
Common pompano, sunfish, pompano
Trachinotus carolinus Linnaeus

SIZE: Reaches a length of 18 inches and weight of 8 pounds.

COLOR: Overall silvery with a golden hue on the head and belly; the caudal fin is dusky or yellow, anal fin yellow to orange.

RANGE: Cape Cod and southward; larger specimens are in the southern part of its range.

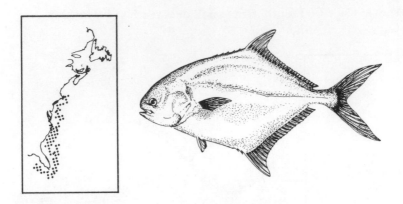

The first dorsal fin has 5 or 6 spines; the second, one spine and from 22 to 27 soft rays. The back is not strongly arched. Adults are toothless.

Pompanos are usually a shallow-water fish. They root about on sandy bottoms for small marine animals.

Pompanos spawn near the shores of the southeastern United States from about May through December.

The epicure rates the pompano high on his list. It is an excellent game fish and it also supports a modest commercial fishery.

Permit
Atlantic permit, round pompano
Trachinotus falcatus Linnaeus

SIZE: Recorded to exceed 50 pounds in weight.

COLOR: Blue to blue-gray back, silvery sides; second dorsal and anal fins may be orange tipped. Young specimens are darker.

RANGE: Cape Cod and southward; most abundant and largest off the Florida coast.

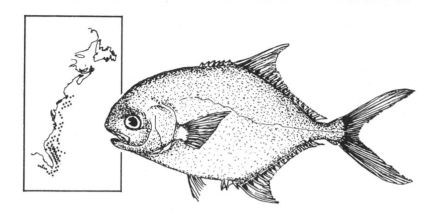

The long rays of its second dorsal and anal fins and its high, arched back distinguish the permit from the pompano (*T. carolinus*).

It is a prize sports fish because of its lightning-fast strike and long runs into the shallows. Large permits present a challenge to even the expert angler.

Spawning occurs during the winter, sometimes as late into the spring as May. The young feed on small marine invertebrates, the adults on larger worms and shellfishes, as well as on small fishes.

Palometa
Longfin pompano, gafftopsail pompano
Trachinotus goodei Jordan and Evermann
Trachinotus glaucus Bloch
Trachinotus palometa Reagan

SIZE: Adult palometa average a foot in length.

COLOR: Silver, darker above; sides are a golden hue with orange breast; long rays on the second dorsal and anal fins are nearly black; narrow vertical bars on the sides.

RANGE: Virginia and southward.

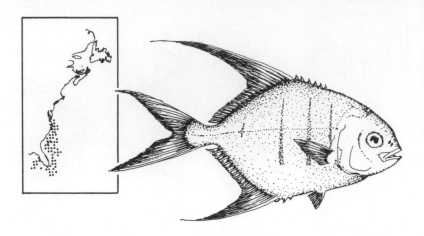

The nose of the palometa is somewhat more pointed than in other pompanos, and the second dorsal, anal, and caudal fins are longer.

Like the permit, the palometa is a coastal fish spending most of its life in the sandy shallows of bays and estuaries.

The palometa is not reported to be as flavorful as other pompanos, but it is definitely edible and sought by sports fishermen.

DOLPHINS — FAMILY *Coryphaena hippurus* Linnaeus

Dolphin
Dorado, common dolphin, Atlantic dolphin
Coryphaena hippurus Linnaeus

SIZE: Dolphins sometimes reach a length of 6 feet, but this is not common.

COLOR: Brilliantly colored; deep blue sides with a strong metallic sheen; golden lower sides and caudal fin.

RANGE: New England southward, straggles to the Maritimes.

The high, blunt forehead, the dorsal fin that is nearly the length of the entire fish, and the deeply forked caudal fin clearly differentiate the dolphin from other fishes in our area.

In tropical waters, the spawning season of the dolphin extends through most of the spring and summer. The young are usually found floating well offshore among patches of sargassum weed. These fish are, of course, not to be confused with the cetaceans also called dolphins.

Dolphins consume a variety of foods, including fishes and shellfishes. They are fast, strong swimmers, which makes them a favorite with sports fishermen. Both their flesh and their roe are considered delicious.

PORGIES — FAMILY *Sparidae*

Scup
Porgy, northern porgy
Stenotomus chrysops Linnaeus
Stenotomus versicolor Mitchill

SIZE: Usually from 12 to 14 inches; those found close inshore are somewhat smaller.

COLOR: A silver fish with iridescent, metallic tones, lighter beneath. Bars on sides disappear rapidly when the fish is taken from the water. The bars are sometimes not present on scup on light sandy bottoms.

RANGE: Mainly from South Carolina to Cape Cod; occasionally found north of Cape Cod.

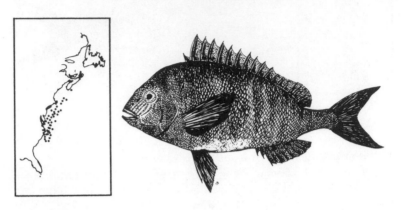

The dorsal fin of the scup is continuous; the caudal fin is moderately forked; the anal fin large; and the pectoral fins sharply pointed. This fish is considerably flattened laterally.

Spawning occurs in the spring, well offshore. Scup feed on a variety of worms and shellfishes and some plant life.

Scup or porgies are among our more popular pan fish, as they are easily caught and are excellent tasting. They are often found around jetties and piers where anyone can fish for them. Their populations, however, are inconsistent. Some years they seem to be everywhere, while in other years they are scarce. They support a significant commercial fishery.

Sheepshead
Archosargus probatocephalus Walbaum

SIZE: Achieves a length of about 20 inches.

COLOR: Silvery, dark above; 5 or more vertical bars; bright silvery sheen on head when fresh.

RANGE: Chiefly from Cape Cod south, sometimes straying somewhat more northward.

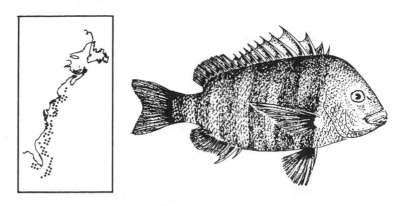

The sheepshead is similar in general appearance to the scup (*S. chrysops*), but it is larger, and its caudal fin is rounded, whereas in the scup it is forked. On the sheepshead the rays of the first dorsal fin alternate in thickness, and the second spine of the anal fin is much thicker than in the scup.

With their strong teeth, sheepshead scrape barnacles off rocks and crush or pick apart clams, mussels, and crabs. They are reported to spawn offshore in the spring.

This is a prized food fish and a prize catch for sports fishermen, as sheepshead are a difficult species to catch.

CROAKER, DRUMS, and WEAKFISHES — FAMILY *Sciaenidae*

Weakfish
Squeteague, sea trout, gray trout, gray weakfish, gray squeteague, yellow fin, tide runner.
Cynoscion regalis Bloch and Schneider

SIZE: Averages 1 to 2 feet in length and 1 to 4 pounds in weight. A 17½-pounder caught on hook and line is on record; a 30-pounder also has been recorded.

COLOR: Olive-green to brown-green above; violet, lavender, green, red, copper, or bronze reflections on back and sides; black, green, or copper blotches and spots on upper sides, forming irregular lines. Dorsal and caudal fins are dusky with yellowish borders; the ventral and anal fins are yellowish.

RANGE: Nova Scotia to Florida; most common from Cape Cod to South Carolina.

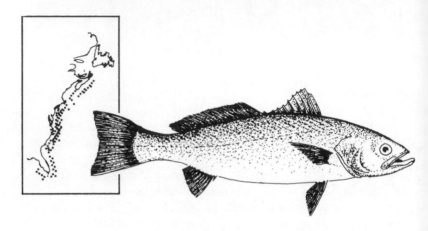

The first dorsal fin of the weakfish is higher than the second and has 10 spines. The caudal fin is slightly emarginate (curved); the anal fin has 2 thin spiny rays and 11 or 12 soft rays. The ventral and pectoral fins are pointed and about the same size. There are 2 sizable canine teeth in the upper jaw.

The diet of weakfish consists of small inshore fishes, as well as shrimps, clams, crabs, and squids. They are schooling fish that roam about bays, estuaries, tidal creeks, and the mouths of rivers, but do not venture into fresh water.

Weakfish are the most commercially important member of the Sciaenidae in our area. They are eagerly sought by sports fishermen as well. Their tender flesh is highly esteemed when properly prepared. The weakfish's mouth parts are weak and the fish sometimes pulls free from the fish hook, giving it its popular name.

Spotted seatrout
Spotted squeteague, southern seatrout, weakfish, spotted weakfish
Cynoscion nebulosus Cuvier

SIZE: A 7-pound spotted squeteague is considered a large specimen.

COLOR: Silver-blue to dark gray above and silver below; upper sides, dorsal and caudal fins are distinctly spotted; fin color is olive or yellow. Young fish have bands.

RANGE: New York and southward.

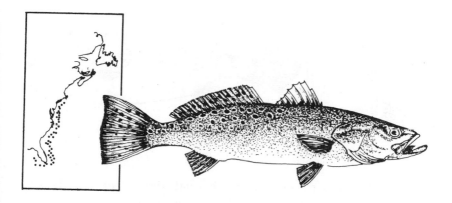

The first dorsal fin of the spotted squeteague* usually has 10 spiny rays and from 24 to 26 soft rays; the anal fin has 2 spiny and 10 or 11 soft rays. The caudal fin is not as concave as in the weakfish (*C. regalis*).

Spawning occurs from March through November in bays and estuaries. The eggs hatch and the young feed in well-vegetated shallows.

Spotted squeteague feed primarily on shrimps but will accept small fishes as well.

This is a valuable sport and commercial fish throughout its range, and it rates high as a food fish.

* Though the American Fisheries Society has designated the name in boldface type as the "official common name," this name is, in the author's opinion, still more widely used.

Banded drum
Banded croaker
Larimus fasciatus Holbrook

SIZE: Reaches a length of 10 inches.

COLOR: Gray to brown-gray with several wide, dark, vertical bands.

RANGE: Chesapeake Bay and southward.

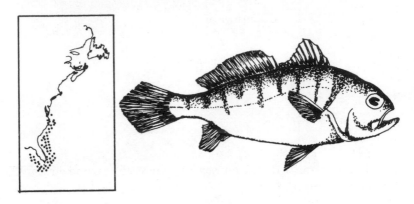

The lower jaw projects beyond the upper and is well toothed. The caudal fin is well rounded (truncate).

The banded croaker* is too small to be of any commercial importance but is a welcome addition as an incidental catch. It is rarely found close to shore.

Spot
Leiostomus xanthurus Lacépède

SIZE: Not common over 12 inches in length; usually 10 inches or less.

COLOR: Blue-gray to gray above; silver lower sides and belly; a distinct dark spot just behind the gills and just above the eyes.

* Though the American Fisheries Society has designated the name in boldface type as the "official common name," this name is, in the author's opinion, still more widely used.

RANGE: Usually Cape Cod and south; reported from the Gulf of Maine. Common New Jersey and southward.

 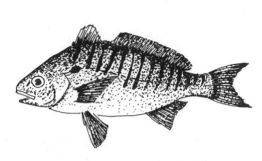

The spot's first dorsal fin has 10 spines; the second has one spine and 30 to 34 soft rays. The anal fin has 2 short, stiff rays and 12 or 13 soft rays. The caudal fin is moderately forked.

The spot is a durable species, tolerating considerable temperature and salinity variations. It is most commonly found in deep water and moves well offshore to spawn.

The spot is easily caught with cut bait, such as worms, quahogs, or clams, and the flesh is considered good table fare.

Red drum
Channel bass, redfish, puppy drum (small fish)
Sciaenops ocellata Linnaeus

SIZE: Reaches a length of over 4 feet; recorded to 83 pounds; common at a third of that weight.

COLOR: Reddish-bronze above and on sides, with a distinct black spot (occasionally 2 or more) at the base of the tail.

RANGE: Cape Cod south, common from New Jersey southward.

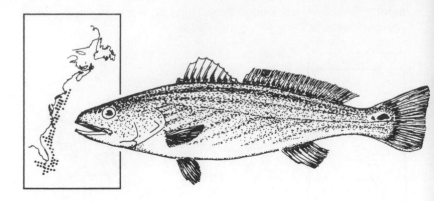

The first dorsal fin of the red drum is slightly higher than the second and contains 11 rays. The caudal fin is emarginate and the upper jaw projects beyond the lower. The fish lacks chin barbels.

Red drum range in depths from tidal flats to over 100 fathoms of water. They subsist on a variety of foods, animal and plant alike. Breeding occurs in deep water in late summer.

The red drum often keeps company with stripers (*Morone saxatilis*) and bluefish (*Pomatom saltatrix*). They are a popular game fish because of their size. The smaller ones, however, are considered better eating.

Black drum
Sea drum
Pogonias cromis Linnaeus

SIZE: A 146-pound black drum has been recorded; those between 20 and 40 pounds are common. The record black drum taken with rod and reel was 4 feet 3 inches in length.

COLOR: Silver with a yellow-copper sheen; may lack the metallic sheen or be reddish, depending upon habitat. Fins are generally darker than the body. Young black drum have bars much like a sheepshead (*Archosargus probatocephalus*). After death the black drum rapidly turns dull in color.

RANGE: Common off New York and southward; occasionally reaches Cape Cod.

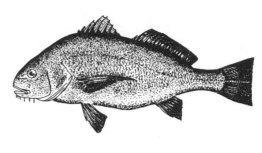

The most distinguishing characteristics of the black drum are its chin barbels, highly arched back, and long, pointed pectoral fins. It has large, distinct scales.

Black drum feed on clams, crabs, and shrimps. They prefer the shallow waters of bays and inlets.

As with other drums, the larger black drum are popular game fish, but the fish is not the best for eating.

Silver perch
Bairdiella chrysura Lacépède

SIZE: Reaches a foot in length, but is usually somewhat smaller.

COLOR: Blue-gray to green-gray above; silver sides; fins are yellowish.

RANGE: Long Island and southward.

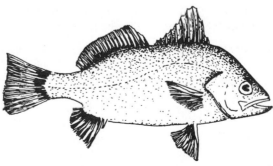

The silver perch may be distinguished from its close relatives by the lateral line which extends the full length of the fish, and by its 2 stiff anal spines. It lacks chin barbels.

The silver perch, though one of the commonest drums, is not well known, as it is not easily caught. It prefers the protected waters of bays and estuaries, and readily ventures into brackish and occasionally into fresh water.

Northern kingfish
Kingfish, king whiting, minkfish
Menticirrhus saxatilis Bloch and Schneider

SIZE: The average northern kingfish is about 1 foot long, though some reach a length of 18 inches.

COLOR: Dull gray to nearly black above; cream-white below; wide vertical bands angling forward on the sides.

RANGE: Common from New York southward; strays to Cape Cod; rare off the Maine coast.

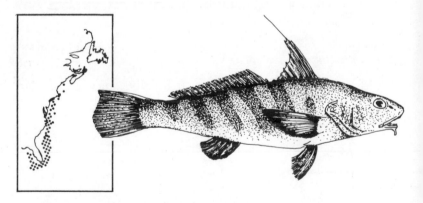

The northern kingfish is easily identified by the long filamentous ray on its first dorsal fin and the S-shaped contour of its caudal fin.

The southern kingfish, *M. americanus,* replaces *M. saxatilis* in the south.

Northern kingfish are present in the summer, coming well inshore in schools. In the late fall they literally disappear, probably retreating to the deeper water where the temperature is more consistent.

Spawning takes place in the summer in shallow water. The young grow to nearly six inches by the first winter.

This is a good table fish and is eagerly sought by sports fishermen.

WRASSES – FAMILY *Labridae*

Wrasses are characterized by a long, continuous dorsal fin and the ventral fins situated directly beneath the pectoral fins.

Cunner
Bergall, perch, chogset
Tautogolabrus adspersus Walbaum

SIZE: Commonly 3 to 6 inches, rarely exceeds 12 inches, but specimens to 15 inches in length have been recorded.

COLOR: Base color is brown, gray-brown, or red-brown to nearly black; lighter belly; bluish tint often beneath the gills; variously marked with red and/or blue spots. Color varies with diet and habitat.

RANGE: Newfoundland to Chesapeake Bay.

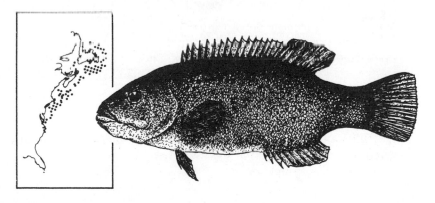

This is a small, hard-bodied, slimy fish that frequents jetties and piers. It has long, sharp teeth with which it deftly steals bait from shore fishermen. It can be distinguished from its close relative, the tautog (*T. onitis*), below, by its more pointed snout, flat forehead, and thinner lips.

The cunner is edible, though quite bony. Its meat is often blue colored, which keeps many people from trying it.

Tautog
Blackfish
Tautoga onitis Linnaeus

SIZE: Recorded to exceed 24 inches in length; specimens half that length and averaging from 2 to 4 pounds in weight are common.

COLOR: Gray-brown to brown, sometimes nearly black, with dark brown or black mottlings on the back and sides; abdomen pale; chin usually light tan to white.

RANGE: Nova Scotia to South Carolina.

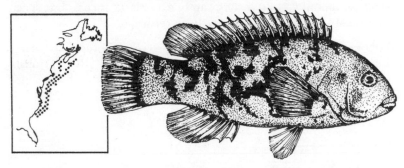

Tautogs can be distinguished by the rounded forehead, very thick caudal peduncle, and thick lips. They have large crushing teeth with which they break open snails, clams, barnacles, and other shelled marine life.

This is an inshore fish, rarely found in the deeper waters of the fishing banks.

The tautog is an excellent fish for eating and is readily marketed, though some people shy away from it because of its tendency to bluish-tinted bones.

MULLETS — FAMILY *Mugilidae*

Mullets are a thick-bodied fish with large scales. They feed primarily on marine vegetation and occasionally on fish eggs or snails.

Striped mullet
Gray mullet, common mullet, mullet
Mugil cephalus Linnaeus

SIZE: 12 to 18 inches long; southern mullet run somewhat larger.

COLOR: Blue-gray, green-gray, or gray above; silver-gray on sides and below; dark spots on scales on upper half of body appearing as longitudinal stripes.

RANGE: Usually from Florida to Cape Cod, occasionally as far north as Nova Scotia.

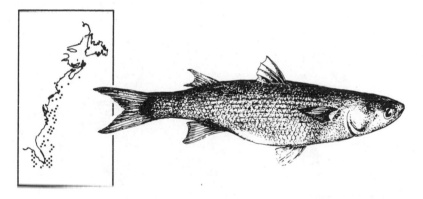

The first dorsal fin of the mullet has 4 spines; the second dorsal, which is well separated from the first, has but one spine and originates over the front of the anal fin. A young mullet is similar to the Atlantic silverside (*M. menidia*) but has a much smaller anal fin. Its scales are large and rounded.

Mullet do not hesitate to venture into brackish and fresh water, where they can be seen taking high leaps out of the water, probably to shake off parasites or for the pure joy of it.

Mullet are not often caught on hook and line as they are primarily vegetarians. They are a good table fish, though not very popular in this country. They are a popular bait fish for sports fishermen.

The striped mullet spawns in the fall when the water temperature is dropping.

White mullet
Silver mullet
Mugil curema Cuvier and Valenciennes

SIZE: Occasionally reaches 3 feet in length.

COLOR: Gray to silver-gray above, slightly lighter on the lower sides and belly.

RANGE: Cape Cod and south; more common in the southern part of its range.

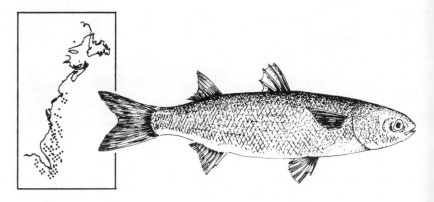

The white mullet has a more rounded head and back than the striped mullet, and achieves a much greater size.

M. curema spawns in the spring on the continental shelf. When the young have grown to about 1 inch in length, they venture inshore.

White mullet are edible but are not often sought for their food value in this country.

BARRACUDAS — FAMILY *Sphyraenidae*

Great barracuda
Barracuda
Sphyraena barracuda Walbaum[14]

SIZE: Known to reach 16 feet in length, but not common over 5 feet.

COLOR: Generally silver with a gray-silver hue above, light silver beneath; dark blotches on the upper sides regularly spaced from gills to caudal fin, mixed with a few irregularly spaced spots. Color varies greatly with size, age, and locale.

RANGE: From the southernmost part of our area north to South Carolina, with stragglers northward to Cape Cod.

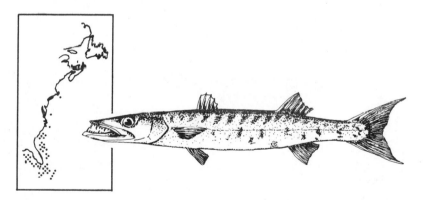

The great barracuda has gained a reputation over the years as a ferocious animal ready to attack at the slightest provocation. Its vicious appearance and a history of inflicting injury on human beings on rare occasion is the basis for this reputation.

This long, slim-bodied fish has two widely separated dorsal fins. The ventral fins are beneath the first dorsal. The mouth is armed with fanglike teeth.

The barracuda is eaten in some tropical countries but its flesh is reported to be toxic on occasion, which makes it a good fish to avoid. Barracuda are popular now with sports fishermen, who release them after capture.

Northern barracuda
Northern sennet
Sphyraena borealis DeKay

SIZE: Rarely exceeds 15 inches in length.

COLOR: Brown-green above; silver sides; white belly; dark vertical bars may be present, particularly on young fish.

RANGE: Cape Cod and south.

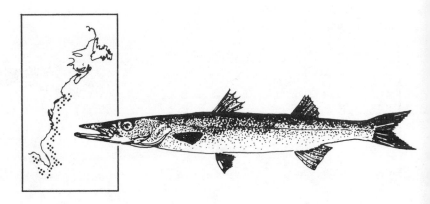

This is the small cousin of the better-known great barracuda. Unlike the great barracuda, it is a fine fish for the table, never reported to be toxic, and where its numbers are great enough it is commercially sought. It lacks the black blotches on the sides that are characteristic of the great barracuda.

GUNNELS — FAMILY *Pholidae*[15]

These are wide-ranging, eellike fishes with extremely long dorsal and anal fins.

Rock gunnel
Rock eel
Pholis gunnellus Linnaeus

SIZE: Averages 7 inches and sometimes 1 foot in length.

COLOR: Yellow-brown, green-brown, or reddish above; the belly a lighter shade of the same color or white. There is a distinctive row of spots on the dorsal fin and there are indistinct bars on the anal fin.

RANGE: Mainly Cape Cod and north, occasionally wanders as far south as Chesapeake Bay.

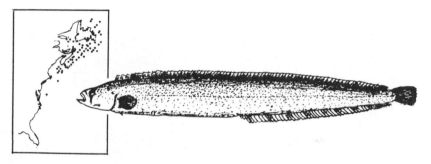

The dorsal fin extends from the gill covers to the base of the caudal fin and the anal fin extends from below the midpoint of the dorsal fin to the base of the caudal fin. The caudal and pectoral fins are rounded, the ventral fins are small and rudimentary. The fish lacks chin barbels.

Rock eels* are found in shallow waters, including tidal pools, but also frequent water up to about 100 fathoms in depth. They feed on a variety of small marine animals including shellfishes, shrimps, and worms.

WOLFFISHES — FAMILY *Anarhichadidae*

Wolffish, or wolf-eels, are long, heavy-bodied fish inhabiting both coasts of North America. *A. lupus* is common in our area.

* Though the American Fisheries Society has designated the name in boldface type as the "official common name," this name is, in the author's opinion, still more widely used.

Atlantic wolffish
Common wolffish, catfish, ocean whitefish
Anarhichas lupus Linnaeus

SIZE: Averages 2 to 3 feet in length, sometimes reaches 5 feet.

COLOR: Generally dark colored, including faint browns, green-browns, or blues; sides have dark bands; the abdomen and throat are an off-white.

RANGE: Mainly from Long Island north; strays as far south as New Jersey.

 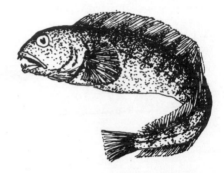

The most obvious distinguishing features of the wolffish are the large, tusklike teeth; the long, high dorsal fin; the lack of ventral fins; and the large, rounded head.

Wolffish have been reported to have bitten bathers and are certainly known to snap viciously at a fisherman when hauled aboard.

A good food fish, they are marketed as catfish and white fish on the East Coast.

WRYMOUTHS — FAMILY *Cryptacanthodidae*

Wrymouths are eel-shaped fishes with large, upturned mouths, long dorsal and anal fins, and no ventral fins.

There are three species in North American waters; *C. maculatus* occurs in our area.

Wrymouth
Ghostfish, congo eel
Cryptacanthodes maculatus Storer

SIZE: Reaches 3 feet in length.

COLOR: Gray-brown, brown, or red-brown with dark spots running the length of the upper half of the body and on the pectoral and anal fins; the belly is nearly white.

RANGE: New Jersey and north; prefers the colder waters.

This unusual-looking fish has the proportional length of an eel but is much more flattened sideways. The entire dorsal fin is spiny and the fish lacks ventral fins. It has a large, upward-turned mouth and an unusually large lower jaw. The dorsal, caudal, and anal fins are continuous, but unlike the eel the wrymouth has distinct indentations at the base of the caudal fin.

The wrymouth is found all the way from the intertidal reaches to water more than 100 fathoms deep.

SAND LANCES (Sand Launces) — FAMILY *Ammodytidae*

The sand launces are a northern family of eellike fishes which inhabit sandy shores, bays, and estuaries.

A. americanus is common on the North American coast. A larger relative, *A. lanceolatus,* which grows to one foot in length, inhabits northern European coasts.

American sand lance
Sand eel, sand lance
Ammodytes americanus DeKay

SIZE: Averages 4 inches or less in length, though recorded to 7 inches.

COLOR: Brown to green-brown with a slight iridescence above, silvery or white beneath; a faint blue stripe may be present along the sides.

RANGE: From the northernmost part of our range south to Cape Hatteras.

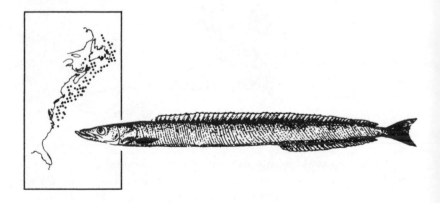

These small shore fish can dig into wet sand to a depth of 6 inches with astonishing speed. This ability keeps them out of sight and helps them escape predators, as well as remain moist when trapped above the low-tide line. They often congregate in large numbers in shallow water. They swim with an eellike motion.

Their distinctly forked tail and separate dorsal, caudal, and anal fins serve to distinguish them from small eels. The dorsal fin extends from just behind the pectoral fin to the caudal peduncle; the anal fin is about one-third as long.

Sand lances subsist largely on small marine animals such as worms and copepods.

MACKERELS AND TUNAS — family *Scombridae*[16]

The mackerels, though varying greatly in size, are all streamlined fishes having one spiny and one soft dorsal fin; both dorsal and anal finlets; and a deeply forked or lunate caudal fin. These fishes are small scaled (seemingly scaleless in some species) and are fast swimmers.

Atlantic mackerel
Common mackerel, mackerel
Scomber scombrus Linnaeus

SIZE: Average size 12 to 13 inches long; some schools run from 14 to 16 inches long; over 16 inches is uncommon.

COLOR: Deep-blue to blue-green, becoming darker, almost black, on the head; sides marked with irregular vertical bars to just below the lateral line; sides and belly silver-white, sometimes with a coppery tinge.

RANGE: Roughly from Labrador to South Carolina; range quite variable from year to year.

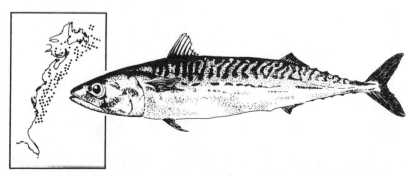

The Atlantic mackerel is, in appearance, typical of the Scombridae. Unlike tunas, however, its tail is forked but not lunate. Mackerel are a fast-swimming fish, as their streamlined shape might suggest. They cannot survive, in fact, without constantly swimming in order to bring a sufficient supply of oxygen to their gills.

Mackerel feed primarily on shrimps, crabs, and small fishes. They rarely disdain any food found in the ocean, a trait which makes them easy to catch with a variety of baits. They are a schooling fish sometimes found in the company of herring.

Mackerel usually spawn during the spring and early summer months. The female may carry half a million eggs as an average. In a year, the fry often reach a length of 8 inches; at this stage they are called "tacks" or "tinkers."

S. scombrus has supported a significant fishery on both sides of the Atlantic throughout history. In spite of being a prolific fish, it is declining in numbers owing to overfishing.

Chub mackerel
Hardhead, tinker
Scomber japonicus Houttuyn
Pneumataphorus colias Gmelin
Scomber colias

SIZE: 8 to 10 inches long, may reach 14 inches.

COLOR: Very similar to the Atlantic mackerel (*S. scombrus*) but the bars on the upper sides are thinner and lighter, and there are mottling and blotches below the lateral line.

RANGE: Nova Scotia to Virginia.

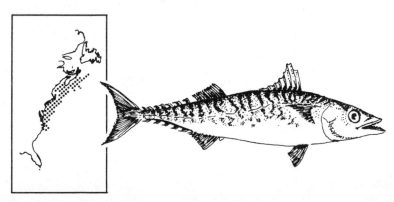

Besides having different markings from the Atlantic mackerel, the chub mackerel may be distinguished by fin ray count. The chub's first dorsal has 9 or 10 spines, whereas there are eleven or more in *S. scombrus*.

Chub mackerel swim in sizable schools and may be found in company with *S. scombrus*. Their diet is substantially the same.

The chub mackerel is an incidental catch along with the Atlantic mackerel, and is not differentiated from it at the market or in restaurants.

Cero
Cavalla, painted mackerel, pintada, king mackerel, kingfish
Scomberomorus regalis Bloch

SIZE: Averages 5–10 pounds; may reach a weight of 35 pounds.

COLOR: Deep blue above, white on lower sides and beneath. A thin brown line runs from the pectoral fins to the caudal fin. There are lengthwise brown markings in rows above and below the lateral line. The first dorsal is dark edged.

RANGE: A southern fish straggling as far north as Cape Cod.

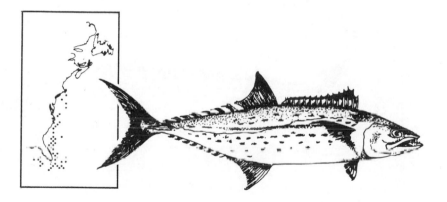

The cero's color most clearly distinguishes it from other mackerels. It is a more slender fish than the king mackerel and has conspicuously more teeth—about 40 to the king mackerel's 30 or so.

The cero is eagerly sought in its southern range as an excellent game fish and for its fine flavor.

King mackerel
Cavalla, kingfish, cero
Scomberomorus cavalla Cuvier and Valenciennes

SIZE: Reaches 5 feet in length and 100 pounds; schools of small king mackerel in 10- to 20-pound range are common.

COLOR: Deep blue to gray above; yellow, cream, or brassy on the sides and beneath. Upper sides have indistinct, wavy vertical bars or gray or yellowish spots becoming weak toward the back of the fish and fading out at approximately the second dorsal fin. Markings are less distinct in older individuals.

RANGE: North Carolina and south; may wander as far north as Cape Cod.

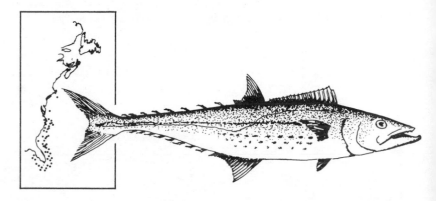

King mackerel feed on a variety of fishes and squids. They are better known in tropical waters as far south as Brazil but wander north often enough to be of interest in our range. They are eagerly sought by sports fishermen both for their high leaps and long, fast runs when hooked, and for their fine-tasting flesh.

Spanish mackerel
Scomberomorus maculatus Mitchill

SIZE: A Spanish mackerel 3 feet long and weighing 10 pounds is an exceptionally large fish; average length is less than 2 feet.

COLOR: Deep blue or blue-green above; silvery cream-white, sometimes with a reddish cast, on sides and below; large oval orange to orange-yellow spots on the sides.

RANGE: Mainly Maryland and southward, occasionally to Long Island; strays to Cape Cod.

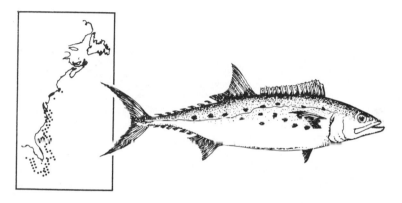

The first and second dorsal fins of the Spanish mackerel are so close together they appear as one. The pectoral fins are scaleless (they are scaled in the cero and king mackerel) and originate distinctly behind the first ray of the dorsal fin. The Spanish mackerel has longitudinal keels on the caudal peduncle, and is a noticeably slimmer fish than most mackerels.

Spanish mackerel feed on menhaden and other small fishes. They travel alone or in small schools.

They are a fine table fish and popular with sports fishermen.

Atlantic bonito
Skipjack, horse mackerel, common bonito
Sarda sarda Bloch

SIZE: Attains a length of 3 feet.

COLOR: Strong blue above; silvery on sides and belly; several (up to 20) fairly straight blue lines running diagonally upward and rearward, none below the pectoral fin.

RANGE: Nova Scotia and southward, more common south of Cape Cod.

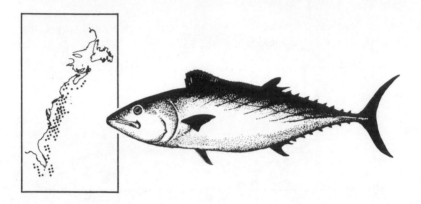

The bonito at first glance looks like a small tuna. Its first dorsal, however, is longer and less concave; also the second dorsal is longer than it is high, whereas in the tunas it is higher than it is long. Bonitos prey upon a variety of small fishes and squids. They spawn well south of the New England coast in the summer months.

Bonitos are powerful fish and fight like a fish many times their size when hooked. They are excellent tasting and may be cooked in a number of ways.

Bluefin tuna
Tunny, tuna, horse mackerel, great albacore
Thunnus thynnus Linnaeus
Thunnus secundodorsalis Storer

SIZE: Exceeds 10 feet in length and one-half ton in weight; recorded at over 1600 pounds.

COLOR: Blue and blue-green to green above; silvery sides and belly; yellow or yellow-brown tones on the sides.

RANGE: Nova Scotia and southward.

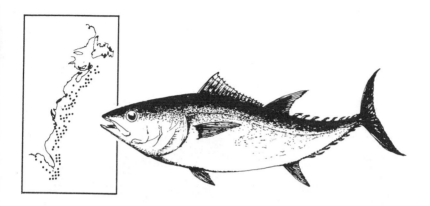

This large offshore tuna wanders close enough toward shore to be caught by small-boat fishermen. The bluefin is a robust fish and a fast swimmer. The entire fish is scaled. Small bluefins may be distinguished from the bonitos and mackerels by their lack of any conspicuous markings.

Bluefin tuna feed primarily on small schooling fishes such as herring and mackerel. They spawn from New England south to Florida during the warmer months.

Bluefins are wide-ranging and are known on both the Atlantic and Pacific coasts. The bluefin has been an important food fish throughout fishing history. It is caught in nets and with hook and line. Sports fishermen consider it a superior game fish.

Yellowfin tuna
Allison's tuna
Thunnus albacares Bonnaterre

SIZE: Usually from 3 to 5 feet; a length of nearly 7 feet has been recorded.

COLOR: The adult yellowfin is deep blue-gray on the top, with golden-yellow streaking on the upper sides; lighter abdomen with white spots and streaks. Small tuna have white vertical lines on the lower sides.

RANGE: Long Island and southward.

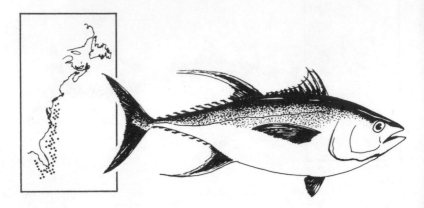

This moderate-sized, colorful tuna is a valuable and widely marketed fish. It is labeled "light meat tuna" as opposed to the white-meated albacore. The Pacific yellowfin supports an international fishery. These tuna can be distinguished by unusually long dorsal and anal fins as well as by their distinctive coloration. Yellowfins eat large quantities of fishes, shrimps, squids, and so on.

Yellowfins frequently swim in large numbers beneath porpoises (dolphins). If purse seines (capture nets) are used to fish for yellowfins, numerous porpoises are also caught and drown before they can be released. New legislation is currently being enacted to limit the methods of net fishing for tuna in an attempt to protect the porpoises.

Albacore
Long-finned tuna
Thunnus alalunga Bonnaterre
Germo alalunga Gmelin

SIZE: To 4 feet long.

COLOR: Steel blue above, silver-white beneath.

RANGE: New Jersey and south, but not common north of Florida.

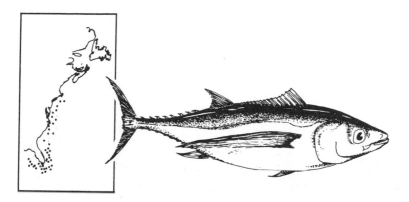

The long pectoral fin clearly distinguishes the albacore from other tunas, as does the narrow white margin on the caudal fin.

Not very common in northern waters, this is the "white-meated" tuna that is so popular. It is caught with hook and line as opposed to yellowfin and bluefin tuna, which are caught by purse seining, which causes the deaths of many, many thousands of porpoises each year.

Albacores feed on fishes, squids, shrimps, and crabs. They support significant fisheries in warm seas throughout the world.

Striped bonito
Ocean bonito
Sarda orientalis Temminck and Schlegel
Gymnosarda pelamis Linnaeus
Euthynnus pelamis Linnaeus

SIZE: Usually from 1½ to 2½ feet long; may reach a weight of 20 pounds.

COLOR: Rich blue above, bright white beneath; approximately 4 blue or brown longitudinal stripes *below* the lateral line.

RANGE: Cape Cod and southward, more common in warmer waters.

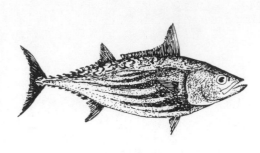

This is an oceanic fish that travels in large schools. It shares with the false albacore (*E. alletteratus*), see below, an unusual band of scales which are in a saddlelike arrangement. These scales are present above the lateral line and down the sides from about halfway along the first dorsal fin to just below the pectoral fins. The striped bonito is the only Scombridae with stripes that are entirely below the lateral line.

These bonito feed on mackerel, menhaden, silversides, and other fishes, and on squid. Ocean bonito spawn in the summer months well south of Cape Cod.

Fishermen seek the striped bonito with hook and line, and it is an excellent food fish.

Little tuna,
False albacore, bonito
Euthynnus alletteratus Rafinesque
Gymnosarda alletterata Rafinesque

SIZE: A length of 2½ feet is unusual for this fish, and it rarely exceeds 3 feet.

COLOR: Deep azure-blue above, creamy and silvery along the

sides, lighter beneath; metallic reflections over the upper half
of the body. Blue longitudinal stripes from the halfway point of
the first dorsal, *above* the lateral line, are squiggly and aimed
slightly upward to the caudal fin.

RANGE: Cape Cod and south; large schools common offshore,
small groups may wander well inshore.

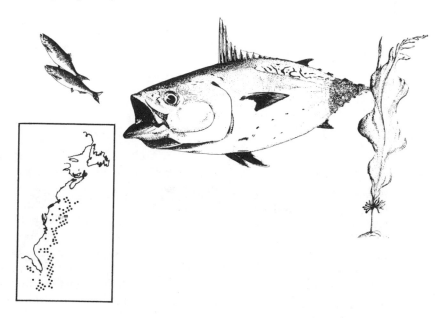

Its markings distinguish the false albacore* from the striped
bonito (*S. orientalis*) and the strongly concave first dorsal fin
distinguishes it from the bonito (*S. sarda*). True tunas have
much longer second dorsal and anal fins.

False albacore feed on fishes, squids, shrimps, and crabs.
They are a prolific fish, the females spawning as many as a million eggs almost any time of the year.

This "little tuna" is particularly attractive and no less than
a superb game fish. It has flavorful, deep red-orange flesh.

* Though the American Fisheries Society has designated the name in boldface
type as the "official common name," this name is, in the author's opinion, still
more widely used.

SWORDFISHES — FAMILY *Xiphiidae*

This family contains one species, X. *gladius,* which is conspicuously characterized by the long, spearlike upper jaw.

Swordfish
Xiphias gladius Linnaeus

SIZE: Reaches 16 feet in overall length.

COLOR: Upper parts dark bluish, grayish, or brownish, white or silvery below. Young have vertical bars.

RANGE: Newfoundland and southward.

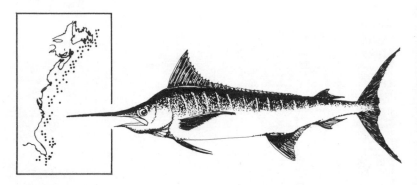

The swordfish is slightly flattened sideways but is generally robust in build, with a slender caudal peduncle. It has an unusually large, gaping mouth extending well beyond the rear margin of the eyes. There are distinct longitudinal keels; a large and a small anal fin; and a high, sharklike dorsal fin. An unmistakable feature is the long, swordlike prolongation of the upper jaw, which gives the fish its name.

Sports fishermen and commercial fishermen alike seek this fish for its fine flavored flesh. Trolling with bait, harpooning, and long-lining are the usual means of capturing it.

Swordfish feed on mackerel, bluefish, menhaden, and a number of other species of fishes, as well as squids if they are available. Swordfish are oceanic, usually dwelling near or on the surface, where their dorsal fins can often be seen as the fish bask. However, they are sometimes caught at great depths.

The sword is a powerful weapon and a live, boated sword-fish should be treated with utmost caution.

MARLINS AND THEIR RELATIVES* —
FAMILY *Istiophoridae*

These are large fishes with an elongated snout and upper jaw. They are principally sought by sports fishermen because of their long runs and spectacular leaps when hooked.

Blue marlin[17]
Skilligalee, spearfish
Makaira nigricans Lacépède
Tetrapterus sp. Jordan and Evermann
Makaira ampla Poey

SIZE: Known to exceed 15 feet in length; over 12 feet is considered very large.

COLOR: Gray-blue on back to about one-third the way down the sides, with a reddish metallic sheen; light gray-blue on sides and beneath; purplish-blue vertical bands on the sides (usually about a dozen).

RANGE: Cape Cod and south; occasionally strays to the coast of Maine, well offshore.

* Referred to as billfishes in some texts.

Blue marlin have the long, spearlike upper jaw and large, luneate caudal fin typical of the marlins and swordfishes. The blue marlin, however, also has a long dorsal fin extending over half the length of the body. Its dark coloration distinguishes it from the white marlin (*M. albidus*).

In our range the blue marlin is considered one of our finest game fish. Farther south, off the Bahamas and in the Carribean, they support a commercial fishery. The blue marlin ranges worldwide.

White marlin
Spearfish
Tetraptera albidus Poey

SIZE: Occasionally exceeds 8 feet in length.

COLOR: Blue and blue-gray to blue-green above; pale sides and white belly; faint vertical bars on upper sides.

RANGE: Cape Cod to Florida, common south of Long Island.

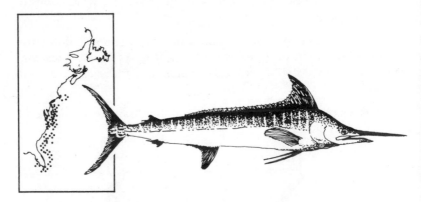

The rounded tips of the dorsal and anal fins differentiate the white marlin from its relatives. The long pectoral and ventral fins are situated beneath one another.

White marlins subsist primarily on other fishes and squids. The white marlin is not as large as many of the favorite game fishes, but a 50-pound fish can be expected and records show specimens exceeding 160 pounds taken by rod and reel. They are not of great food value and most of them are released.

Atlantic sailfish
Sailfish
Istiophorus platypterus Shaw and Nodder
Istiophorus americanus Cuvier and Valenciennes

SIZE: Full-grown Atlantic sailfish are from 6 to 8 feet in length.

COLOR: Deep blue to steel blue above; silver-white sides and belly; faint, thin vertical stripes. Southern specimens may show a copper or golden tinge.

RANGE: The warm Atlantic north to Cape Cod; common in the southern part of its range.

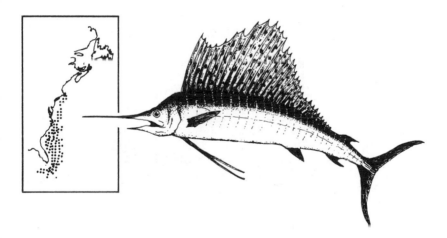

The enormous dorsal fin is the unmistakable field mark of the sailfish. It has, as well, exceptionally long ventral fins, which are situated directly beneath the pectoral fins.

Sailfish spawn in the summer. Ripe females may carry over 4 million eggs. Young sailfish grow rapidly, reaching a length of 4½ feet and a weight of 6 pounds in 6 months.

This is a widely sought game fish but not generally prized for its food value.

BUTTERFISHES (Harvestfishes) — FAMILY *Stromateidae*

Barrelfish[13]
Black rudderfish, black pilotfish
Hyperoglyphe perciformis Mitchill
Palinurichthys perciformis Mitchill

SIZE: Reaches a length of from 12 to 14 inches.

COLOR: Generally a very dark green-brown to black overall, sometimes with a paler belly with small dots.

RANGE: Nova Scotia south to Cape Cod.

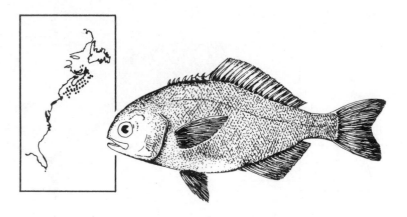

The first rays of the first dorsal fin of the barrelfish are short and widely spaced, followed by a long, fairly even, soft-rayed second dorsal fin. Its snout is rounded.

The barrelfish has a habit of hanging around floating planks or drifting wreckage, or even following slow-moving vessels, a habit to which it owes its alternate name, black rudderfish.

Barrelfish feed on barnacles, mussels, squids, and so forth, which they find near or attached to their floating homes.

H. perciformis is not very common or commercially sought after.

Butterfish
Dollarfish, harvestfish
Peprilus triacanthus Peck
Poronotus triacanthus Peck

SIZE: Reaches a length of 12 inches, commonly 6 to 9 inches.

COLOR: Dull silver-blue above, silver beneath. Fresh specimens may show faint spots.

RANGE: Nova Scotia to South Carolina.

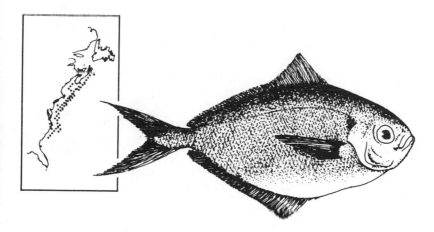

The butterfish is extremely flattened laterally, and disk shaped. The dorsal and anal fins are nearly the same length. The caudal fin is deeply forked.

Butterfish prefer warmer waters and north of Maryland are present in numbers only in mid to late summer.

Butterfish feed on a variety of foods, including fishes, squids, shrimps, and worms.

A significant commercial fishery exists for the butterfish, owing to their excellent flavor. They are usually harvested in pound nets, trawls, or purse seines.

Harvestfish
Peprilus alepidotus Linnaeus

SIZE: Averages 6 to 9 inches in length.

COLOR: Generally silvery, greenish hue on the back, frequently a golden tinge on the sides.

RANGE: Florida to Virginia, straggles north to Cape Cod.

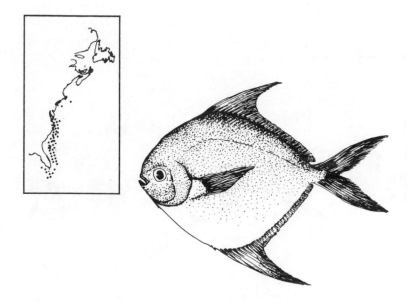

This close relative of the butterfish may be distinguished by the long first rays of the dorsal and anal fins and its overall rounder appearance.

Harvestfish are a highly sought-after food fish. They are often caught and marketed along with butterfish.

SCORPIONFISHES OR ROCKFISHES — FAMILY *Scorpaenidae*

These perchlike fishes are really close relatives of the sculpins and sea robins. They are characterized by bony plates on the head with spines on the cheeks (opercula). They are represented in our area by the redfish, *S. marinus.*

Redfish
Rosefish, Atlantic rockfish, ocean perch, red sea perch, red bream, Norway haddock, red perch
Sebastes marinus Linnaeus

SIZE: From 10 to 20 inches in length, but rarely exceeds 18 inches.

COLOR: Orange, orange-red, or bright red; in certain environments appears dull brown or gray-red. Lighter beneath, dark blotches on the gill covers and back (very faint or missing on some fish).

RANGE: Newfoundland to New Jersey.

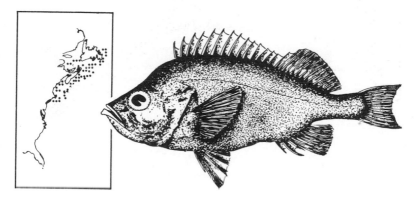

The spiny and soft dorsal fins are continuous; the caudal fin is slightly concave; the anal fin is preceded by 3 stiff rays; and the gill covers are pointed. There are a number of spines on the gill cover.

Redfish breed in cold water (below 40° F) and the females hold the fertile eggs until hatching. The young dwell on the surface for their first year of life. Adults feed primarily on other fishes.

The redfish is a valuable food fish but is usually marketed under the names of sea perch or red perch, which are actually unrelated fishes.

SEAROBINS — FAMILY *Triglidae*

Searobins are sculpinlike fishes with heads wholly covered with a bony plate.

Northern searobin
Common searobin, Carolina searobin
Prionotus carolinus Linnaeus

SIZE: Averages about 1 foot in length, but may exceed 16 inches.

COLOR: Red-brown or gray-brown with several dark bands over the back and partly down the sides; abdomen nearly white, often with a yellowish tinge; fins are striped; free rays of the pectoral fin are distinctly yellow to orange.

RANGE: South Carolina and northward; not very common north of Cape Cod.

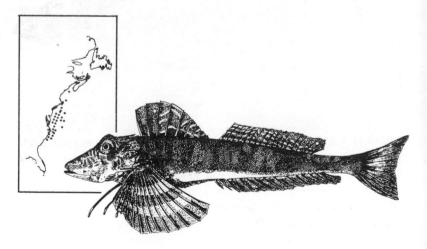

The searobin has a bony plate covering the entire head, with 4 spines; a mildly concave caudal fin; and large, fanlike pectoral fins with 3 free, fleshy rays preceding each fin. Out of the water, searobins emit a grunting or barking sound. Searobins are warm-water fish and usually spend the colder months well out to sea on the continental shelf.

Though considered a nuisance by most fishermen, the sea-robin is a fine fish for eating and is also a popular lobster bait.

Striped searobin
Prionotus evolans Linnaeus

SIZE: Reaches about 18 inches in length.

COLOR: Narrow dark bars on the sides, orange or brown pectoral free rays; otherwise quite similar to the northern searobin (*P. carolinus*).

RANGE: Usually from South Carolina to Cape Cod; occasionally rounds the Cape.

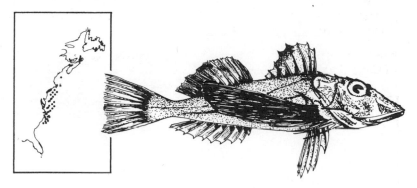

To distinguish this searobin from *P. carolinus,* look for gen-erally longer fins, particularly the pectorals, which extend back to beyond the halfway point of the second dorsal fin; a nearly straight caudal fin; and a flatter head.

Striped searobins prefer shallow waters, where with the aid of the free rays of the pectoral fin, they forage about on the bottom in search of small marine animals.

SCULPINS* — FAMILY *Cottidae*

This is a large family of both marine and freshwater species, found in a variety of environments and climates.

Arctic hookear sculpin
Hookear sculpin, Atlantic sculpin
Artediellus uncinatus[18] Reinhardt

SIZE: Does not commonly exceed 4 inches in length.

COLOR: Brown, gray-brown, or reddish-brown on a lighter background; caudal fin usually banded.

RANGE: From the northernmost reaches of our range to Cape Cod.

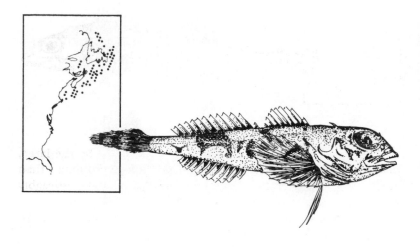

The hookear sculpin is a small cold-water fish. It has large, bulging eyes and lacks scales. The upturned spines on the gill covers give the fish its name. The jaws and the roof of the mouth are armed with small bristly teeth.

The hookear sculpin is found in water up to 200 fathoms deep, but never in large numbers.

* Referred to as "cottids" in some texts.

Mailed sculpin
Triglops nybelini Jensen
Triglops ommatistius Gilbert

SIZE: A 6-inch mailed sculpin is the longest recorded in our area.

COLOR: Gray-green to olive-green above, yellow to orange beneath; 4 dark blotches on each side.

RANGE: Rarely reaches as far south as Cape Cod.

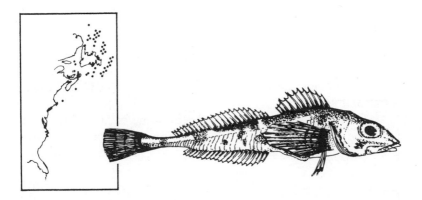

The mailed sculpin can be easily distinguished by the large, platelike scales on its sides. Overall it appears slimmer than other sculpins. The first dorsal fin is higher and noticeably shorter than the second and contains from 10 to 12 spines.

Mailed sculpins favor the icy-cold waters of the North Atlantic.

Grubby
Little sculpin
Myoxocephalus aenaeus Mitchill

SIZE: Rarely exceeds 7 inches in length.

COLOR: Green-gray, gray, or brown-gray above, mottled on the sides, whitish beneath.

RANGE: Nova Scotia south to New Jersey.

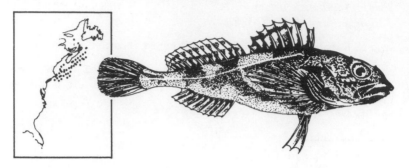

This is one of the smaller common sculpins in the colder waters of our range. It has short cheek spines, 9 spines in the first dorsal fin, 13 or 14 rays in the second dorsal fin, and 10 or 11 rays in the anal fin.

The grubby is too small to be of commercial value. It is somewhat of a nuisance to hook-and-line fishermen as it bites greedily at nearly any bait.

Shorthorn sculpin
Greenland sculpin, black sculpin
Myoxocephalus scorpius Linnaeus

SIZE: Averages 1 foot and reaches 2 feet in length.

COLOR: Red-brown to gray-brown or black-brown above, light blotches on back and sides, abdomen marked with cream-yellow (female) or orange (male) spots.

RANGE: Mainly Cape Cod and north; strays south to Long Island on occasion.

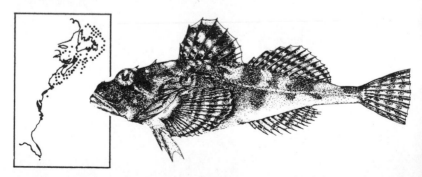

This is our largest sculpin and one of the most common. It tolerates a wide range of temperatures but prefers cold water.

The shorthorn is distinguished from other sculpins by 13 or 14 anal fin rays and a deep pore behind the gill cover on the throat.

It is edible but its ungainly appearance makes it less than popular as a table fish. Out of water, the shorthorn often makes grunting sounds much like the sea robin.

Longhorn sculpin
Gray sculpin, toadfish
Myoxocephalus octodecemspinosus Mitchill

SIZE: Averages less than 1 foot in length, may reach 18 inches.

COLOR: Varies in color depending on habitat; ranges from brown-green to yellow-green on back and sides. There are indistinct or irregular crossbars; the first dorsal fin is grayish with blotches; the second is pale gray-green with three irregular bars; the caudal fin is grayish; the anal fin is dull yellow. The belly is nearly white.

RANGE: Mainly Newfoundland to New Jersey; strays somewhat southward.

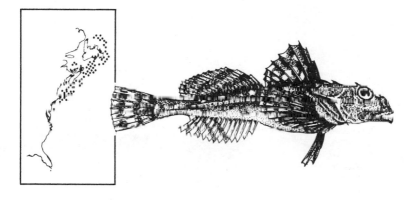

The longhorn may be distinguished from the shorthorn (*M. scorpius*) by the long naked spines on the gill covers. It is also a slimmer fish.

This is a fish of the shoal waters but it rarely enters brackish water. It prefers temperatures as high as 65° F but can tolerate near-freezing temperatures.

Longhorns spawn during the winter months off the New England coast.

Longhorn sculpins are edible fish, but as with so many sculpins, their appearance denies them the popularity of other table fish.

Sea raven
Sea sculpin, red sculpin
Hemitripterus americanus Gmelin

SIZE: Averages a little over 18 inches in length; specimens to 25 inches have been recorded.

COLOR: Red to red-violet to brown above, paler sides, belly cream to yellow; fins are variously marked. Colors vary with age and habitat.

RANGE: South to Cape Cod, strays to Chesapeake Bay.

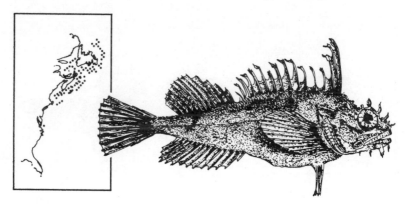

The first part of the first dorsal fin of the sea raven has 4 rays and the second, 12. There are 12 rays in the second dorsal fin. Its mouth is well toothed and the skin is covered with small spines.

The sea raven is a good fish for eating despite its appearance. It makes excellent lobster bait as well.

POACHERS (Alligator Fishes) — FAMILY *Agonidae*

This family is characterized by nonoverlapping bony plates. It ranges in both the Pacific and Atlantic oceans.

Alligatorfish
Poacher, sea poacher, Atlantic poacher
Aspidophoroides monopterygius Bloch

SIZE: Averages 6 inches in length, rarely exceeds 7 inches.

COLOR: Dark gray-brown above, tan below; indistinct bands from the dorsal fin back; bars on the second dorsal and caudal fins.

RANGE: South to Cape Cod, strays to New Jersey.

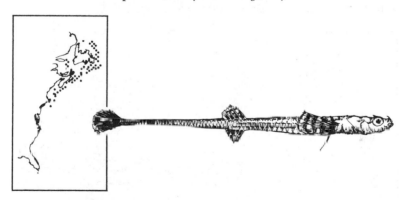

Instead of having scales of the usual type, the slim-bodied alligatorfish is covered with longitudinal rows of bony plates. It prefers cold waters, avoiding waters much above 52° F.

LUMPFISHES — FAMILY *Cyclopteridae*

Lumpfish
Lumpsucker
Cyclopterus lumpus Linnaeus

SIZE: Usually less than 16 inches in length; recorded above 20 inches.

COLOR: Various blues and browns on top and sides, belly lighter, dark blotches or spots on sides; males have a bright red abdomen during the breeding season.

RANGE: Newfoundland south to New Jersey.

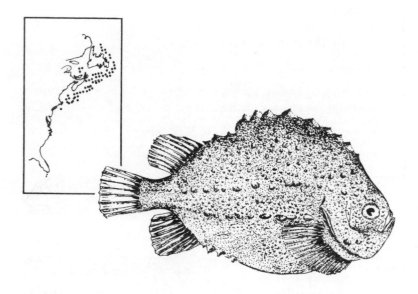

The lumpfish stands out from other fishes in our area by its odd appearance. Identifying characteristics include the sharp lumps or tubercules; the rearward position of the dorsal fin, which is directly over the anal fin; a bony sucking disk on the chest; and a small mouth.

FLYING GURNARDS — FAMILY *Dactylopteridae*

Flying gurnard
Dactylopterus volitans Linnaeus

SIZE: Rarely exceeds 12 inches in length.

COLOR: Brown to green-brown above; yellow or orange-yellow marks on lower sides; pectoral fins show blue bars and dots; caudal fin has red-brown to brown vertical bars.

RANGE: Mainly North Carolina and south, strays as far north as Cape Cod in late summer.

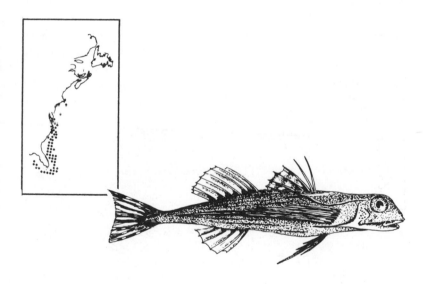

With the enormous pectoral fins, which reach as far back as the caudal peduncle, the free rays of the first dorsal fin, and an unusually blunt forehead, the flying gurnard is not easily confused with any other fish in our range. There is also a bony plate on either side of the top of the head and at the base of the gill cover, extending back beyond the origin of the first dorsal fin, and terminating in a spine.

FLATFISHES
(FLOUNDERS AND SOLES)
ORDER *Pleuronectiformes* (Heterosomata)

FAMILIES *Pleuronectidae, Bothidae,* and *Soleidae* (Achiridae)

This order of fishes has flat bodies with both eyes on the same side of the head, a unique characteristic among the orders of fishes. They are bottom fishes, ranging in size from a few inches to several feet in length.

The flounders are actually not flattened fishes, but rather fishes that swim on their side. As hatchlings, flounders look like any other fish, but as they pass from the larval stage to adulthood, one eye migrates around the head to join the other. In some species the left eye will migrate around to the right side of the fish (dextral), in other species the right eye will migrate to the left side (sinistral).

Flounders are of tremendous economic importance. Species such as the yellowtail of the North American continental shelf, and the halibuts of the North Atlantic and Pacific oceans support substantial industries.

"Right-handed" flounders (Pleuronectidae) include the following species:[19]

> GREENLAND HALIBUT, *Reinhardtius hippoglossoides*
> ATLANTIC HALIBUT, *Hippoglossus hippoglossus*
> AMERICAN PLAICE, *Hippoglossoides platessoides*
> YELLOWTAIL, *Limanda ferruginea*
> WINTER FLOUNDER, *Pseudopleuronectes americanus*
> WITCH FLOUNDER, *Glyptocephalus cynoglossus*
> SMOOTH FLOUNDER, *Liopsetta putnami**

"Right-handed" flounders (Soleidae) include the following species:

---

* Names followed by asterisks indicate that these fish were considered too scarce or too far out of our range to be included in this volume.

HOGCHOKER, *Trinectes maculatus*
STRIPED SOLE, *Achirus lineatus**

"Left-handed" flounders (Bothidae) include the following species:

SUMMER FLOUNDER, *Paralichthys dentatus*
FOURSPOT FLOUNDER, *Paralichthys oblongus*
WINDOWPANE, *Lophopsetta maculata*
GULF STREAM FLOUNDER, *Citharichthys arctifrons**
EYED FLOUNDER, *Platophrys ocellatus**
PEACOCK FLOUNDER, *Platophrys lunatus**
SPOTFIN FLOUNDER, *Cyclopsetta fimbriata**
SMALLMOUTH FLOUNDER, *Etropus microstomus**
BAY WHIFF, *Citharichthys spilopterus**

Greenland halibut
Greenland turbot
Reinhardtius hippoglossoides Walbaum

SIZE: May exceed 3 feet in length and 20 pounds in weight; 10-pounders are common.

COLOR: Gray-brown, sometimes with a yellow tint above; very light brown beneath.

RANGE: Occurs only in the northernmost part of our range.

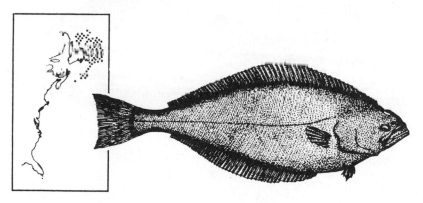

The Greenland halibut is easily mistaken for the Atlantic halibut, but it has a straight lateral line and the mouth is larger in proportion to the size of the animal. It is an excellent fish for eating and is comparable to the Atlantic halibut in economic value, though it is far less commonly caught.[19] Markets generally distinguish it by labeling it "turbot."

Atlantic halibut
Halibut
Hippoglossus hippoglossus Linnaeus

SIZE: The Atlantic halibut is the largest of the flounders. Record specimens exceed 700 pounds in weight, but individuals of more than 300 pounds are uncommon.

COLOR: Green-brown, occasionally grayish above; white below, with gray blotches in older individuals. Young Atlantic halibut show some mottling above.

RANGE: From the northernmost part of our range south to Chesapeake Bay, rarely farther south. Most abundant in the Gulf of Maine and northward.

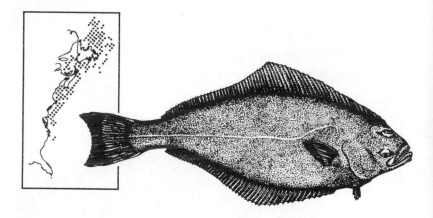

In addition to its size, the Atlantic halibut can be identified by the large mouth, which extends to the middle of its eyes; a distinct arch in the lateral line over the pectoral fin; and a concave caudal fin.

Atlantic halibut prefer sandy bottoms between 30 and 500 fathoms, avoiding rocky or muddy conditions. They are voracious feeders, preying on a variety of fishes such as cod, haddock, perch, flounders, and mackerel, as well as lobsters, crabs, and shellfishes. They are, in turn, prey to seals and the Greenland shark.

They are a prolific species, but overfishing and disturbing of their bottom environment have countered this natural characteristic. A large adult female may carry more than 2 million eggs.

Once a fish of major commercial importance, the Atlantic halibut is now, though welcome at the table, becoming an incidental catch. For the sports fisherman it is perhaps more important, as it puts up an admirable fight once hooked.

American plaice
Sand dab, American dab, Canadian plaice
Hippoglossoides platessoides Fabricius

SIZE: Usually from 1 to 2 feet; rarely exceeds 30 inches in length.

COLOR: Rusty gray-brown above; white below.

RANGE: Mainly from Nova Scotia to Cape Cod, occasionally straying south of the Cape.

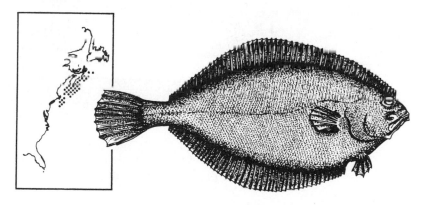

The American plaice can be identified by its large mouth, rounded caudal fin, and almost straight lateral line.

These are usually bottom fish, preferring sandy and soft bottoms in a wide range of depths. Their diet consists chiefly of small marine invertebrates such as shrimps and crabs. Only occasionally do they catch fishes.

An excellent table fish, they are commercially important as an incidental catch.

Yellowtail flounder
Rusty flounder, Rusty dab
Limanda ferruginea Storer

SIZE: Average size is 15 to 18 inches; the female grows noticeably larger than the male.

COLOR: Brown to olive-brown with large, irregular orange to orange-red spots; fins margined in yellow. The brighter colors rapidly fade upon death.

RANGE: From Nova Scotia to Chesapeake Bay, most common in the central portion of this range.

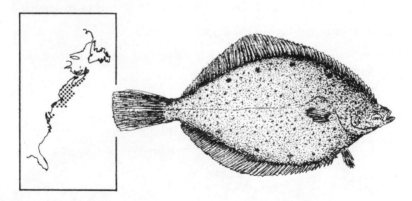

The yellowtail is one of the most important species supporting the commercial fisheries of the northeastern United States. It is commonly trawled for at depths of from 20 to 50 fathoms.

It can be distinguished by its color, particularly the yellow margins on the fins; its small mouth; a rather long, pointed snout; and a thin body.

The yellowtail prefers sandy and hard muddy bottoms, avoiding rocky areas. It feeds on shrimps, small shellfishes, and other small invertebrates.

Winter flounder
Blue-back flounder, black-back flounder, lemon sole, black flounder, snowshoe, gray sole
Pseudopleuronectes americanus Walbaum

SIZE: Averages 12 to 15 inches in length, rarely exceeds 20 inches.

COLOR: Dark brown, gray-brown, sometimes reddish or olive hued, often spotted; white on the underside.

RANGE: Nova Scotia south to Georgia.

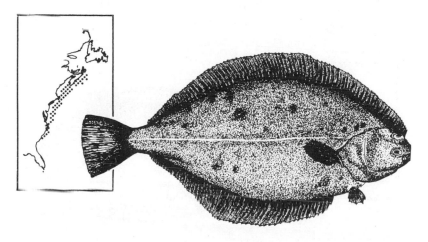

The winter flounder has a small mouth and small, rough scales on the eye side, and is smooth on the blind side. The dorsal fin is fairly even throughout its length; the pectoral fin is small; the tail is slightly rounded.

In the warmer months, winter flounder retreat into deeper, cooler waters. In the spring they return to the shallows, where the female lays up to one-half million eggs on sandy bottoms in water below 40° F. In a year the young grow to as much as six inches in length.

At one time this flounder was caught in large numbers in the spring along the jetties and wharfs, while on its way to the spawning grounds in the shallows and marshes. Today its numbers have been greatly reduced by overfishing and pollution.

Witch flounder
Gray sole, Pole flounder
Glyptocephalus cynoglossus Linnaeus

SIZE: From 12 to 24 inches long; weight to 4 pounds.

COLOR: Brown to brown-gray, sometimes with faint transverse bars; white underneath.

RANGE: In deeper water from as far south as North Carolina northward along the continental shelf to the Maritimes.

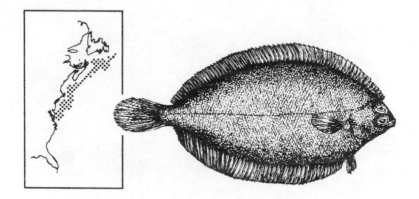

The witch flounder most closely resembles the winter flounder. It can be distinguished by its proportionately smaller head; proportionately smaller and more rounded caudal fin; and approximately 12 large mucous pits on the blind side. The dorsal and anal fins are about equal in width. It is a thinner fish than the winter flounder.

The witch flounder is rarely encountered in less than 10 fathoms of water and ranges out to depths of over 150 fathoms. It is an excellent table fish but commercially important only as an incidental catch.

Hogchoker
American sole
Trinectes maculatus Bloch and Schneider
Achirus fasciatus Lacépède

SIZE: Rarely exceeds 8 inches in length.

COLOR: Gray-brown, olive-brown, or dark brown with 7 or 8 dark brown vertical stripes; distinct, dark brown lateral line; off-white on the blind side.

RANGE: Cape Cod south, plentiful from Long Island south to North Carolina.

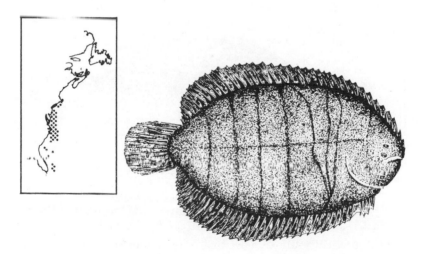

This small sole ranks high on the gourmet's list. It is not likely to be confused with any other flounder because of its distinctly rounded shape. It has a very small mouth and lacks a pectoral fin, and the ventral fin is continuous with the anal fin. It is a shoal-water fish, rarely venturing into deep water.

Summer flounder
Fluke

SIZE: A 3- to 5-pound summer flounder is a respectable catch. In rare instances they reach 3 feet in length and 15 pounds in weight.

COLOR: The chameleon of flounders, the summer flounder takes on the color of the bottom, occasionally adding blues, greens, browns, and black spots or blotches of its own. The average summer flounder is of a brown hue with dark spots.

RANGE: Chiefly from the southern part of the Gulf of Maine to South Carolina, straying as far south as Florida.

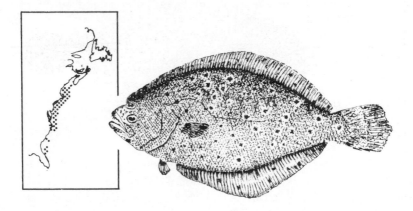

The summer flounder has a well-toothed, gaping mouth; an arched lateral line; and a rounded caudal fin. The left ventral fin is not continuous with the anal fin.

These fish quickly leave the northern waters when the water temperature drops in the fall, and thereafter are in evidence only south of Long Island.

The summer flounder can be easily caught by drift-fishing, providing enjoyment for the angler as well as furnishing a good meal. In the summer, when they come inshore, they are often caught by small commercial fishing boats using drag nets.

Fourspot flounder
Paralichthys oblongus Mitchill

SIZE: From 10 to 14 inches.

COLOR: Dark gray, slightly mottled, with four distinct, pink-edged eye spots; off-white on the blind side.

RANGE: From the northern part of our range south to North Carolina; common from Cape Cod to New Jersey.

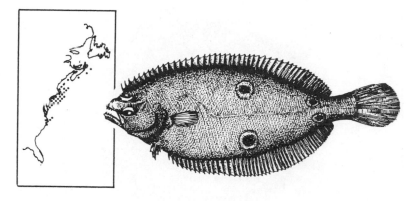

The fourspot flounder is well described by its common name. It is an incidental catch for both amateur and commercial fishermen, but is valued by both because of its fine flavor. Only occasionally are these flounder caught in shallow waters, as they normally range in depths of between 17 and nearly 170 fathoms.

Windowpane
Sand flounder, spotted flounder, sundial
Scophthalmus aquosus Mitchill
Lophopsetta maculata Mitchill

SIZE: To 18 inches and 2 pounds, 12-inch specimens are common.

COLOR: Green-brown to olive-brown, sometimes with a rusty overtone, marked with many irregular dark brown spots. The fins have the same markings as the body. (*Note:* The windowpane apparently will cross with other flounders, resulting in a variety of colors and shapes.)

RANGE: From the northern part of our range south to Cape Cod, and sometimes plentiful south of the Cape in the summer.

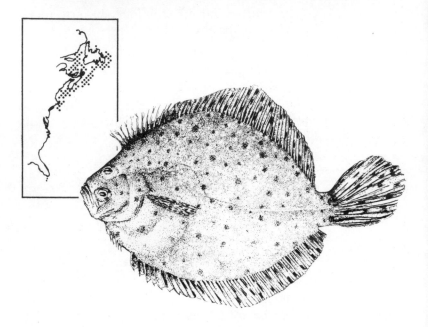

The most distinctive feature of the windowpane is the separated rays on the front portion of the dorsal fin. The ventral fin is separate from the anal fin. This fish has a large mouth and a fully rounded caudal fin.

The windowpane is commercially important only as an incidental catch but it provides good fishing fun for the amateur fisherman in relatively shallow water, as well as excellent food fare.

ORDER *Tetraodontiformes* (Plectognathi)

FILEFISHES AND TRIGGERFISHES — FAMILY *Balistidae*

The Balistidae are a family of sidewise-flattened fishes with the first ray of the dorsal fin strongly modified as a triggerlike projection that can be locked in place at will, or as a separate (adipose) rough ray or spine.

Planehead filefish
Common filefish, filefish
Monacanthus hispidus Linnaeus

SIZE: Reaches a length of about 10 inches.

COLOR: Green, green-brown, or brown; the dorsal spine and caudal fin are green; the second dorsal and anal fins are translucent. Young ones show a dark mottling on the back and sides.

RANGE: North to Cape Cod, reported from Nova Scotia.

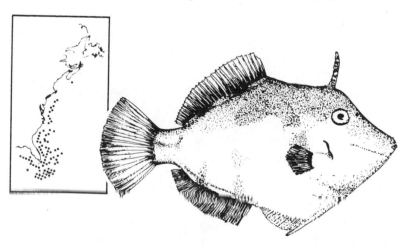

The first dorsal fin of the planehead filefish takes the form of a heavily barbed spine. The caudal fin is rounded. (In the triggerfish it is concave.) The mouth is very small and well toothed. The anal fin is situated directly beneath the second dorsal and is of the same shape, but without any prolonged rays. The small pectorals are directly behind and slightly beneath the slitlike gill openings.

Orange filefish
Turbot, unicornfish, sunfish
Aluterus schoepfi Walbaum

SIZE: Reaches a length of 2 feet.

COLOR: Variously colored; may be orange, yellow-orange, gray-green, green, or nearly white, blotched with various hues on upper sides; abdomen blue-white; caudal fin yellowish.

RANGE: Mainly Cape Cod and south, but strays to Nova Scotia.

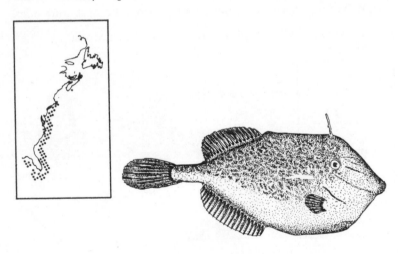

The orange filefish can be distinguished from other filefishes by its smooth abdomen; long-rayed, rounded second dorsal and anal fins; very small eyes; and small, well-toothed, and upward-turned mouth. The pectoral fins are situated beneath and extend partially behind the oblique gill slits.

Gray triggerfish
Common triggerfish, northern triggerfish
Balistes capriscus Gmelin
Balistes carolinensis Gmelin

SIZE: Does not usually exceed 1 foot in length.

COLOR: Varies somewhat, but is commonly green-gray with yellow spots; fins yellowish.

RANGE: Nova Scotia south, but rare north of Cape Cod and not common anywhere north of the warm seas off Florida and Georgia.

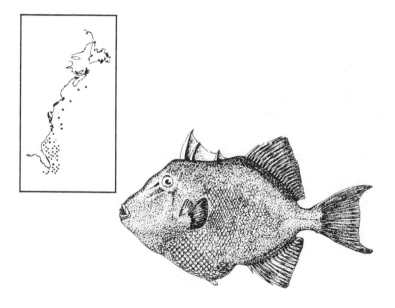

One is not likely to confuse this fish with any other in our area. The unique first spine of the first dorsal fin is long, very sharp, and can be raised and locked into place by the second ray. The body of the fish is covered by hard, bony scales.

Triggerfishes are not considered edible, as many of the various species are somewhat toxic. The dorsal spine can cause a very painful puncture wound and should be carefully avoided.

PUFFERS — FAMILY *Tetraodontidae*

Northern puffer
Puffer, swellfish, balloonfish, globefish
Sphoeroides maculatus Bloch and Schneider

SIZE: Averages 8 to 10 inches, but sometimes reaches 15 inches in length.

COLOR: Yellow-brown, sometimes with a greenish tinge above; yellow-green to orange on the sides; belly white; back is variously blotched; sides are marked with irregular crossbars.

RANGE: Mainly from Florida to Cape Cod, but reaches Nova Scotia as a straggler. Not consistent in its distribution, often abandoning areas where it was formerly abundant.

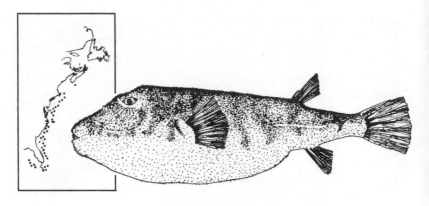

The most distinctive feature of this fish is its habit of filling with air or water when disturbed, its abdomen becoming nearly globular. When filled with air, it will float, and if left undisturbed will suddenly deflate and dive beneath the surface.

The puffer's single dorsal and anal fins are placed well back on the body so as to be nearly on the caudal peduncle. The eyes are small and the mouth has large, flat "buck" teeth. The skin is sandpapery in texture.

Puffers are abundant in some regions from time to time, but

may be scarce in the same areas at other times. They feed on small crabs, shrimps, mollusks, and other marine invertebrates. They are prolific, spawning from Chesapeake Bay to Cape Cod throughout the summer.

The puffer is an excellent table fish, as there is a large strip of sweet, tender meat on either side of the backbone.

PORCUPINE FISHES — FAMILY *Diodontidae*

Striped burrfish
Burrfish, porcupinefish, rabbit fish
Chilomycterus schoepfi Walbaum

SIZE: Reaches a length of 10 inches.

COLOR: Green-brown to olive with dark brown stripes running laterally along the sides; belly lighter with a yellow-orange tinge. There is a large dark spot below the dorsal fin.

RANGE: Mainly from Florida north to southern Long Island, with strays to Cape Cod.

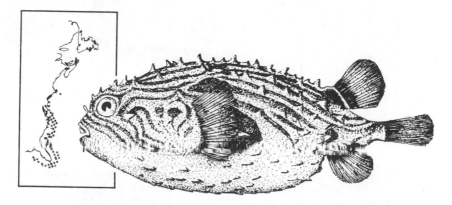

The most distinctive features of this member of the porcupinefish family are the firm triangular spines all over its body;

the dorsal and anal fins, which are situated on the caudal peduncle; the fanlike pectoral fin; and the small mouth, armed with large wedge-shaped teeth.

MOLAS OR SUNFISHES — FAMILY *Molidae*

Ocean sunfish
Sunfish, headfish
Mola mola Linnaeus

SIZE: Grows to a length of 8 or more feet and a weight of nearly 1 ton.

COLOR: Gray to gray-brown above; silver-gray sides; gray-white beneath.

RANGE: A tropical species wandering as far north as the coast of New England.

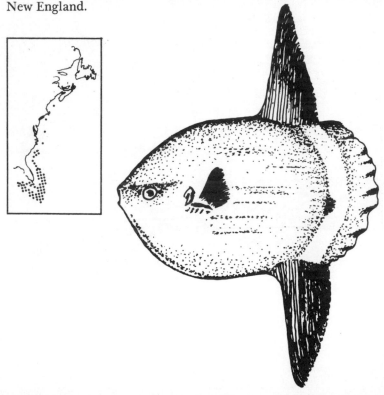

The ocean sunfish is best described as a large head with a tail fin. Its size and shape alone distinguish it from all other fish in our range save the sharptail mola (*M. lanceolatus*) from which it differs by having a pointed projection on the middle of the caudal fin instead of an evenly scalloped outline.

The meat of the ocean sunfish is not particularly palatable, leaving it to be not much more than a curiosity of the oceans.

POSSIBLE HAZARDS IN HANDLING FISHES

FISH	INJURY	CAUSE	PREVENTION
Barracudas	Bite, poisoning.	Large razor-sharp teeth, toxic viscera.	Handle live fish carefully; keep children away. Do not eat viscera or roe.
Billfish and spearfish	Slash wounds from thrashing fish.	Sharp bills (beaks), sharp edges of the caudal peduncle and caudal fin.	Do not boat live fish without proper experience and equipment; keep children away.
Bluefish	Flesh wounds from bites.	Freshly caught fish snap at anything with their long, sharp teeth.	When removing hooks or handling, use gloves or pliers.
Conger eel	Bites.	Inconspicuous teeth.	Handle with care and with gloves.
Goosefish	Bites.	Lies on bottom in shallow water with very large, well-toothed mouth wide open and bites anyone that steps on it.	Do not allow very young bathers to wade about where large goosefish are common.
Halibut	Slash wounds from thrashing fish.	Sharp caudal peduncle and base of caudal fin.	Kill or stay clear of freshly caught or large fish.
Needlefish	Stab wounds.	Long sharp bill. When disturbed at night they may leap long distances.	Duck!!!
Puffers	Poisoning.	Viscera and roe can be toxic.	Avoid eating viscera or roe.
Sand shark	Bites, poisoning.	Apparently docile fish may bite if provoked; liver is toxic.	Do not disturb basking fish; children should not swim where they are prevalent. Unhook fish carefully. Do not eat liver.

POSSIBLE HAZARDS IN HANDLING FISHES (Cont'd)

FISH	INJURY	CAUSE	PREVENTION
Sculpins and relatives	Stab wounds, toxic reactions to viscera.	Numerous spines on body; toxic viscera and roe.	Handle carefully; do not eat viscera or eggs.
Scup	Punctures.	Sharp spines on fins.	Handle carefully and with gloves when removing hook.
Sea basses	Puncture wounds.	Sharp spines on fins and gill rakers.	Handle live fish carefully. When grasping fish by gills, remove fingers carefully.
Searobins	Poisoning.	Eggs are toxic.	Do not eat eggs.
Sharks	Bites.	Razor-sharp teeth in the larger sharks.	Handle only with proper equipment and experience.
Spiny dogfish	Puncture wounds, poisoning.	Sharp spines ahead of dorsal fins; liver toxic.	Handle carefully, avoiding dorsal fins; do not eat liver.
Stargazer	Severe puncture wounds.	Sharp, toxic spines on dorsal fin.	Avoid any contact with dorsal fin.
Stingrays	Severe and painful puncture wounds.	Spine or spines on back and/or tail.	Avoid contact with spines. Live rays may lash out with tail.
Toadfish	Bites and puncture wounds.	Sharp teeth and body spines.	Handle with extreme care; can cause severe wounds.
Triggerfish	Severe puncture wounds.	Erectile spine ahead of the dorsal fin.	Avoid contact with spine.

NOTES

1. A member of Family Lamnidae, mackerel sharks, in American Fisheries Society Special Publication No. 6, 1970.
2. Credited to Valenciennes by American Fisheries Society Special Publication No. 6, 1970.
3. The smooth dogfishes are included in Family Carcharhinidae, requiem sharks, in American Fisheries Society Special Publication No. 6, 1970.
4. True bone by definition is permeated with canaliculi (*Haversians canals*), which are absent in sharks, skates, and rays.
5. Included as members of Order Clupeiformes in some texts.
6. Argentines have, in the past, been classified in their own family, Argentinidae.
7. The Greenland cod, *G. ogac*, is recognized in some texts.
8. Hakes are assigned their own family, Merlucciidae, by some authorities.
9. *M. menidia* is broken down into two races in some texts: *M. m. menidia* Linnaeus, which averages 40 lateral-line scales, and *M. m. notata* Mitchill, which averages 46 lateral-line scales.
10. The actual twospine stickleback is another species (*G. whaetlandi* Putnam), also called the black-spotted stickleback.
11. Families Serranidae and Percichthyidae were separated by W. A. Gosline in 1966 so as to include certain marine basses.

12. The Cuban jack is a misnamed species in some texts, e.g., National Geographic Society, *Wondrous World of Fishes,* 1965, page 110.
13. *H. perciformis* has a number of local names, creating some confusion. The common name given here is based on the American Fisheries Society Special Publication No. 6, 1970.
14. Authority for *S. barracuda* is attributed to Shaw in some texts.
15. Family Pholidae is grouped with families Lumpenidae and Stichaeidae as "blennylike" fishes in some texts.
16. An alternate classification of the Scombridae is Suborder Scombriodes.
17. *Tetrapterus sp.* and *Makaira sp.* are treated as separate species by Jordan and Evermann, California Academy of Science, Occ. Papers XII, page 28, 1926.
18. *A. uncinatus* Reinhardt is differentiated from a separate species, *A. atlanticus* Jordan and Evermann, in recent reports.
19. On rare occasions individuals are encountered that are "right-handed" when they should be "left-handed" and vice-versa.

BIBLIOGRAPHY

American Fisheries Society. *A List of Common and Scientific Names of Fishes from the United States and Canada.* Special Publication No. 6. 3d ed. Washington, D.C., 1970.

BIGELOW, HENRY B., and SCHROEDER, WILLIAM C. *Fishes of the Gulf of Maine.* Washington, D.C.: Government Printing Office, 1953.

BREEDER, CHARLES M. *Field Book of Marine Fishes of the Atlantic Coast.* Rev. ed. New York: Putnam, 1948.

BRIDGES, WILLIAM. *Book of the Water World.* New York: American Heritage, 1970.

BROOKES, R. *The Natural History of Fishes and Serpents.* London: Bible and Sun at St. Paul's Church-yard for J. Newbery, 1763.

COLLINS, HENRY H., JR. *Complete Field Guide to American Wildlife.* New York: Harper, 1959.

COOPER, ALLAN. *Fishes of the World.* New York: Grosset and Dunlap, Inc., 1971.

HARDY, SIR ALLISTER. *The Open Sea, Its Natural History.* Boston: Houghton Mifflin, 1970.

HERALD, EARL. *Fishes of North America.* New York: Doubleday,

HICKSON, SIDNEY J. *The Story of Life in the Seas.* University Society, 1909.

IDYLL, C.P., ed. *Exploring the Ocean World.* New York: Crowell, 1972.

Larousse Encyclopedia of Animal Life. New York: McGraw-Hill, 1967.

LORD ROTHSCHILD. *A Classification of Living Animals.* London: Longmans, 1961.

MCCLANE, A.J., ed. *McClane's Standard Fishing Encyclopedia.* New York: Holt, Rinehart, 1965.

MCCLANE, JOHN F. *Checklist of the Fishes of New Jersey.* Trenton, N.J.: Bureau of Fisheries, New Jersey Department of Environmental Protection, 1975.

MARSHALL, N.B. *Explorations in the Life of Fishes.* Cambridge, Mass.: Harvard University Press, 1971.

MARSHALL, NORMA, and MARSHALL, OLGA. *Ocean Life.* New York: Macmillan, 1971.

MIGDALSKI, EDWARD G. *Boy's Book of Fishes.* New York: Ronald, 1964.

MUGFORD, PAUL S. *Massachusetts Freshwater Fish.* Boston: Massachusetts Division of Fisheries and Game, 1969.

National Geographic Society. *Wondrous World of Fishes.* Washington, D.C.: 1965.

SPOTTE, STEPHEN H. *Fish and Invertebrate Culture.* New York: Wiley, 1970.

WEYL, PETER K. *Oceanography.* New York: Wiley, 1970.

WHEELER, ALWYNE. *Fishes of the World, An Illustrated Dictionary.* New York: Macmillan, 1975.

WHITLEY, GILBERT, and ALLAN, JOYCE. *The Sea Horse and Its Relatives.* Melbourne, Australia: Georgian House, 1958.

WOOLNER, FRANK. *Modern Salt Water Fishing.* New York: Crown, 1972.

ZIM, HERBERT S., and SHOEMAKER, HURST H. *Fishes, A Guide to Familiar American Species.* New York: Golden, 1955.

INDEX TO COMMON NAMES

INDEX TO SCIENTIFIC NAMES

striatus, Centropristes, 144
Stromateidae, 204
sturio, Acipenser, 72
symmetricus, Trachurus, 156
Syngnathidae, 138
Syngnathus fuscus, 139

Tarpon atlanticus, 75
tau, Opsanus, 106
taurus, Carcharias, 35
taurus, Odontaspis, 35
Tautoga onitis, 180
Tautogolabrus adspersus, 179
tenuis, Phycis, 113
tenuis, Urophycis, 113
teres, Etrumeus, 81
terraenovae, Rhizoprionodon, 42
terraenovae, Scoliodon, 42
Tetraodontidae, 232
Tetraodontiformes, 229
Tetraptera albidus, 202
Thoracostei, 134
Thunnus alalunga, 196
Thunnus albacares, 195
Thunnus secundodorsalis, 194
Thunnus thynnus, 194
thynnus, Thunnus, 194
tiburo, Sphyrna, 49
tigris, Isurus, 38
tomcod, Microgadus, 108
Torpedinidae, 55
Torpedo nobiliana, 55
Trachinotus carolinus, 165
Trachinotus falcatus, 166
Trachinotus glaucus, 167
Trachinotus goodei, 167
Trachinotus palometa, 167
Trachurops crumenophthalmus, 155
Trachurus lathami, 156
Trachurus symmetricus, 156
Trachurus trachurus, 156

trachurus, Trachurus, 156
triacanthus, Peprilus, 204
triancanthus, Poronotus, 204
Triakidae, 47
Triglidae, 208
Triglops nybelini, 211
Triglops ommatistius, 211
Trinectes maculatus, 225
trutta, Salmo, 95
tyrannus, Brevoortia, 89

uncinatus, Artediellus, 210
unifasciatus, Hyporhamphus, 121
Urophycis chester, 115
Urophycis chuss, 114
Urophycis regius, 112
Urophycis tenuis, 113

variegatus, Cyprinodon, 129
versicolor, Stenotomus, 169
villosus, Mallotus, 99
virens, Pollachius, 110
volitans, Dactylopterus, 217
vomer, Selene, 164
Vomer setapinnis, 164
vulpes, Albula, 76
vulpes, Alopias, 41
vulpinus, Alopias, 41

xanthurus, Leiostomus, 174
Xiphias gladius, 200
Xiphiidae, 200

Zeidae, 132
Zeiformes, 132
Zenopsis ocellata, 132
Zeomorphi, 132
Zeomorphi, 133
Zoarcidae, 118
zonata, Seriola, 162
zygaena, Sphyrna, 49

ABOUT THE AUTHOR

Naturalist, wildlife artist and photographer, Michael J. Ursin, though born in Oslo, Norway, has lived for many years in New England and is an expert on the life of our oceanic and coastal waters, estuaries and marshes, rivers and lakes. Formerly publisher and editor of *World Wildlife* magazine, his home and studio are in Holden, Massachusetts, and on Martha's Vineyard. Michael J. Ursin is also author of *Life In and Around the Salt Marshes* and *Life In and Around Freshwater Wetlands,* and has contributed many articles and illustrations to journals and magazines.

NOTES

NOTES

NOTES